POWERS OF ATTORNEY AC

Second Edition

AUSTRALIA
Law Book Co.
Sydney

CANADA and USA
Carswell
Toronto

HONG KONG
Sweet & Maxwell Asia

NEW ZEALAND
Brookers
Wellington

SINGAPORE AND MALAYSIA
Sweet & Maxwell Asia
Singapore and Kuala Lumpur

POWERS OF ATTORNEY ACT 1996

Second Edition

Brian Gallagher

B.C.L., Solicitor

DUBLIN
ROUND HALL SWEET & MAXWELL
2001

Published in 2001 by
Round Hall Ltd
43 Fitzwilliam Place
Dublin 2

Typeset by
Gough Typesetting Services
Dublin

Printed by
Genprint (Ireland) Ltd

ISBN 1-85800-230-3

A catalogue record for this book
is available from the British Library.

*All rights reserved. No part of this publication may
be reproduced or transmitted in any form or by any means,
including photocopying and recording,
without the written permission of the publisher.
Such written permission must also be obtained before any
part of this publication is stored in a retrieval system
of any nature.*

©
Round Hall Ltd
2001

POWERS OF ATTORNEY ACT, 1996

(1996 No. 12)

ARRANGEMENT OF SECTIONS

PART I

PRELIMINARY AND GENERAL

SECT.
1. Short title and commencement.
2. Interpretation generally.
3. Statutory declaration by company.

PART II

ENDURING POWERS OF ATTORNEY

4. Interpretation.
5. Characteristics of enduring power.
6. Scope of authority of attorney under enduring power.
7. Coming into force and survival of enduring power.
8. Functions of court prior to registration.
9. Application for registration.
10. Registration.
11. Effect and proof of registration.
12. Functions of court with respect to registered power.
13. Protection of attorney and third person where registered power invalid or not in force.
14. Application to joint and joint and several attorneys.

PART III

POWERS OF ATTORNEY GENERALLY

15. Creation of power.
16. Effect of general power in specified form.
17. Execution of instruments, etc. by donee of power.
18. Protection of donee and other persons where power revoked.
19. Protection of transferee under stock exchange transaction.
20. Power given as security.
21. Proof of instrument creating power.
22. Deposit of original instruments in Central Office.
23. Furnishing to purchaser of power relating to land.

PART IV

MISCELLANEOUS

24. Laying of orders and regulations before Houses of Oireachtas.
25. Repeals.

Powers of Attorney Act 1996

FIRST SCHEDULE

Notification prior to Registration

SECOND SCHEDULE

Joint and Joint and Several Attorneys

THIRD SCHEDULE

Form of General Power of Attorney

FOURTH SCHEDULE

Enactments Repealed

An Act to provide for powers of attorney to operate when the donor of the power is or is becoming mentally incapable and to amend in other respects the law relating to powers of attorney generally. [5*th June*, 1996]

Introduction and General Note

The object of this legislation is twofold: first, to provide for a new legal creature called "an enduring power", a power of attorney which, with certain exceptions, comes into force when it has been registered under section 10 of the Act, and is not revoked by the donor's subsequent mental incapacity; and secondly, to make certain amendments to the law relating to powers of attorney generally.

It was not possible to create an instrument with the characteristics of an enduring power prior to the commencement of the Act. The commonly understood power of attorney came (and still comes) into effect on execution, and lasts (and continues to last) until death, revocation or the onset of mental incapacity. The problem with the commonly known power of attorney was (and is) that it ceases to have effect when the donor becomes mentally incapable. Both the enduring power and the commonly known power of attorney cease on the death of a donor.

Enduring powers are a phenomenon of the late twentieth century. They were introduced in England and Wales by the Enduring Powers of Attorney Act 1995 (c. 29), and are provided for in many other common law jurisdictions, for example in the United States of America, Canada, Australia and New Zealand. For those interested in a detailed study of enduring powers, working papers or reports have been issued by the Law Reform Commissions of, for example, Ontario, British Columbia, Australia, Manitoba and Newfoundland, quite apart from the work which has been done by the U.K. Law Commission. For a detailed report on the workings of the United Kingdom Enduring Powers of Attorney Act 1995, see the report prepared by the Faculty of Law, University of Bristol for the Lord Chancellor's Department in June 1991.

The Powers of Attorney Bill 1995 was initially introduced in Seanad Éireann when the Minister for Equality and Law Reform stated that it was:

> "An important social measure, the purpose of which is to allow persons to put in place arrangements for managing their affairs in the event that they should become mentally disabled." (144 *Seanad Debates* Col. 1241.)

In restating the law as it existed at that time he said that:

> "When a person becomes mentally incapable and the question of managing his or her affairs arises, the only option under the existing law is to have that person made a ward of court. Wardship can be a complex, time-consuming and expensive procedure." (*ibid*.)

The wards of court jurisdiction of the courts is not affected in any way by the Act.

The Minister referred to the incidence of Alzheimer's disease, stating that it was believed that there are more than 25,000 Irish *adult* sufferers, who may be as young as 50, 40, or even 30 years of age. Concluding his opening comments, the Minister stated that:

> "Mental incapacity can also result from brain injury at any age, perhaps most commonly from road accidents. The existence of a power of attorney which would not be revoked on the occurrence of mental incapacity would act as a kind of insurance against the effects of accidental injuries of this kind. In fact in jurisdictions where enduring powers of attorney have been introduced, many young people have executed these enduring powers as a precaution against such an eventuality". (144 *Seanad Debates* Col. 1242.)

In dealing with Part III of the Act the Minister said that it was "concerned with updating the law on powers of attorney generally" (144 *Seanad Debates* Col. 1247). While mentioning sections 15 and 16 particularly, the Minister characterised the remaining sections in Part III as being "of a technical nature and . . . best left for consideration on committee stage" (*ibid.*).

The Act had an uncontroversial passage through the Oireachtas, but quite a number of amendments were made to the initial Bill, necessitating its return to Seanad Éireann after passage by Dáil Éireann. Many of these amendments were brought about as a result of representations made by the Law Society of Ireland and the Dublin Solicitors Bar Association.

Commencement

The Act was signed by the President on June 5, 1996 and came into force pursuant to S.I. No. 195 of 1996 on August 1, 1996.

Statutory Instruments

Powers of Attorney Act, 1996 (Commencement) Order 1996 (S.I. No. 195 of 1996)
Enduring Powers of Attorney Regulations 1996 (S.I. No. 196 of 1996)
Enduring Powers of Attorney (Personal Care Decision) Regulations 1996 (S.I. No. 287 of 1996)
Rules of the Superior Courts (No. 1) (Powers of Attorney Act 1996), 2000 (S.I. No. 66 of 2000)

Acts Referred to

Companies Act, 1990	1990, No. 33
Conveyancing Act, 1881	1881, c. 41
Conveyancing Act, 1882	1882, c. 39
Health (Nursing Homes) Act, 1990	1990, No. 23
Lunacy Regulation (Ireland) Act, 1871	1871, c. 22
Settled Land Act, 1882	1882, c. 38
Stock Exchange Act, 1995	1995, No. 9
Stock Transfer Act, 1963	1963, No. 34
Succession Act, 1965	1965, No. 27

Be it enacted by the Oireachtas as follows:

Part I

Preliminary and General

Short title and commencement

1.—(1) This Act may be cited as the Powers of Attorney Act, 1996.

(2) This Act shall come into force on such day or days as the Minister shall

appoint by order or orders either generally or with reference to any particular provisions and different days may be so fixed for different provisions.

Interpretation generally

2.—(1) In this Act, unless the context otherwise requires—

"convey" includes transfer, lease and assign, and "conveyance" shall be construed accordingly;

"power" means power of attorney;

"power of attorney" means an instrument signed by or by direction of a person (the donor), or a provision contained in such an instrument, giving the donee the power to act on behalf of the donor in accordance with the terms of the instrument;

"statutory declaration" includes a statutory declaration made in accordance with section 3.

(2) (*a*) In this Act a reference to a Part, section or Schedule is a reference to a Part, section or Schedule of this Act unless it is indicated that reference to some other enactment is intended.

(*b*) In this Act a reference to a subsection, paragraph or subparagraph is a reference to the subsection, paragraph or subparagraph of the provision in which the reference occurs unless it is indicated that reference to some other provision is intended.

(3) In this Act a reference to an Act is to that Act as subsequently amended.

GENERAL NOTE

Section 2 is an interpretation section for the purposes of the Act. The original definition of "power of attorney" in the Bill was amended. As originally defined, "power of attorney" meant "an instrument signed by or by direction of a person (the donor) and by the donee (or by each donee if more than one) giving the donee or donees the power to Act on behalf of the donor in accordance with the terms of the instrument". The definition as originally drafted would have imposed an additional requirement in relation to *all* powers of attorney; that they be signed by the donee as well as the donor. (Enduring Powers must, however, be signed by both donor and donee.)

Prior to this enactment there were no special provisions in Ireland governing the creation of a power of attorney. (Sections 7 and 8 of the Conveyancing Act 1882 dealt with the irrevocability of powers of attorney.) The rule at common law was that it had to be done by deed (see *R. v. Martin* (1831) Glasc. 33). In the case of a corporation, the requirements of its memorandum and articles of association, *e.g.* in relation to affixing its seal, had to be met (see *O'Connor v. Bernard* (1842) 4 Ir. Eq. R. 689).

Statutory declaration by company

3.—Where, for any purpose of this Act, a statutory declaration is to be made by a person being a corporation aggregate it may be made on behalf of the corporation by a person authorised by the corporation to act on its behalf.

GENERAL NOTE

Section 3 facilitates the making of statutory declarations for any purposes of the Act where the statutory declaration has to be made by a company, *e.g.* for the purposes of sections 13(4) or 18(4).

Part II

Enduring Powers of Attorney

Interpretation

4.—(1) In this Part—

"affairs", in relation to a donor of an enduring power, means business or financial affairs of the donor;

"attorney" means the donee of an enduring power and includes a person acting in pursuance of section 5(3) and complying with the provisions of this Act and regulations made thereunder;

"the court" means the High Court;

"enduring power" shall be construed in accordance with section 5(1);

"mental incapacity", in relation to an individual, means incapacity by reason of a mental condition to manage and administer his or her own property and affairs and cognate expressions shall be construed accordingly;

"the Minister" means the Minister for Equality and Law Reform;

"notice" means notice in writing;

"personal care decision", in relation to a donor of an enduring power, means a decision on any one or more of the following matters:

(a) where the donor should live,
(b) with whom the donor should live,
(c) whom the donor should see and not see,
(d) what training or rehabilitation the donor should get,
(e) the donor's diet and dress,
(f) inspection of the donor's personal papers,
(g) housing, social welfare and other benefits for the donor;

"registration", in relation to an enduring power of attorney, means registration under section 10, and "registered" shall be construed accordingly.

(2) An application or reference to the court under this Part shall be made in a summary manner.

(3) If any question arises under this Part as to what the donor of the enduring power might at any time be expected to do it shall be assumed that the donor had the mental capacity to do so.

GENERAL NOTE

This section is an interpretation section for the purposes of Part II of the Act. Important government amendments were made to the section as originally worded in the Bill. The first amendment was the insertion of a definition of "affairs". The word "affairs" is used in section 6 (below), and the amendment was intended to restrict its interpretation. Representations had been made by, *inter alia*, the Law Society of Ireland and the Dublin Solicitors' Bar Association that the Act should empower the donee of an enduring power to make what are later termed "personal care decisions" on behalf of a donor. This power was not included in the Bill as introduced. It was argued that on one interpretation the word "affairs" could extend to personal care decisions. It seems, therefore, that by introducing the provision to empower a donee specifically to make certain personal care decisions it was decided specifically to restrict the meaning of the word "affairs" to the "business or financial affairs" of the donor.

The definition of "attorney" was amended to include substitute attornies appointed under section 5(3). "The court" is defined as the High Court. There was considerable parliamentary debate in relation to this, and in particular Mr Michael Woods, T.D., the Fianna Fáil Spokesman on Equality and Law Reform, pressed the Minister quite strongly to change "the court" to the Circuit Court (465 *Dáil Debates* Col. 1133). However, despite the arguments of the Opposition, "the court" remained as the High Court. The Act is, however, not as clear as it might be in relation to whether applications for the registration of an enduring power should be made to a judge of the High Court or to the Registrar of Wards of Court.

In a Practice Direction (see Appendix C below) which was made by the President of the High Court after the Act had come into operation, it was provided that applications for the registration of enduring powers should, in effect, be made to a Judge of the High Court, by means of the issuing of a special summons. This Practice Direction has been supplanted by S.I. No. 66 of 2000 (See Appendix D below).

In this connection it is interesting to see that the Minister for Equality and Law Reform stated to the Dáil that registration of the enduring power would be "done in the office on an administrative basis". And "it is rather similar to the Probate application procedures" (465 *Dáil Debates* Cols. 1134–1135).

The definition of "mental incapacity" as meaning "incapacity by reason of a mental condition" is now seen as being possibly problematical. A practical problem has arisen in relation to people suffering from strokes. They may suffer from very serious physical, but in many cases not mental incapacity.

The definition of "personal care decision" was not in the original Bill and was introduced after representations were made by, *inter alia*, the Law Society of Ireland and the Dublin Solicitors Bar Association. Many of those making representations sought to have the definition specifically extend to medical treatment. However, this seems to have been regarded as too much of a 'hot potato' and the Act does not empower the donee to make decisions regarding the donor's medical treatment. Thus, the attorney of a person in a permanent vegetative state does not, it appears, have power, nor can he or she be given power to terminate medical intervention (see commentary on Guidelines on Treatment Decisions for Patients in Persistent Vegetative State in (1996) 2(2) *Medico-Legal Journal of Ireland* 57).

Section 4(2) did not appear in the Bill as introduced. (See comments above in this note on the definition of "the court"). Section 4(3) originally contained the phrase, "unless the contrary is shown", after the word "assumed". This subsection can be connected to section 6(4) and (5) which refer to matters which the donor might be expected to do. For example, section 6(4) empowers an attorney under an enduring power to act in relation to the attorney or another person to provide for his or her or that persons needs, respectively, "if the donor might be expected" to do so. Presumably, it was thought necessary to ensure that the expectation of the donor would be looked at objectively, and not challenged subjectively on the grounds of the donor's lack of mental capacity.

Characteristics of enduring power

5.—(1) A power of attorney is an enduring power within the meaning of this Act if the instrument creating the power contains a statement by the donor to the effect that the donor intends the power to be effective during any subsequent mental incapacity of the donor and complies with the provisions of this section and regulations made thereunder.

(2) The Minister may make provision by regulations in relation to all of the following matters concerning enduring powers of attorney:

    (a) their form,

    (b) their execution,

    (c) ensuring that any document purporting to create an enduring power incorporates adequate information as to the effect of creating or accepting the power,

    (d) the inclusion in the document of all of the following statements—

(i) by the donor, that the donor has read the information as to the effect of creating the power or that such information has been read to the donor,

(ii) by a solicitor (or a member of some other specified class of persons), that, after interviewing the donor and making any necessary enquiries, the solicitor or such member—

(I) is satisfied that the donor understood the effect of creating the power, and

(II) has no reason to believe that the document is being executed by the donor as a result of fraud or undue pressure,

(iii) by a registered medical practitioner, that in his or her opinion at the time the document was executed the donor had the mental capacity, with the assistance of such explanations as may have been given to the donor, to understand the effect of creating the power,

(iv) by the attorney, that the attorney understands the duties and obligations of an attorney and the requirements of registration under section 10,

(e) the keeping of accounts by the attorney in relation to the management and disposal of the donor's property,

(f) the remuneration, if any, to be paid to the attorney,

(g) the attestation of the signatures of the donor and the attorney,

(h) specific provision for cases where more than one attorney is appointed,

(i) the giving by the donor to specified persons of notice of the execution of the power, and

(j) if the regulations amend or revoke any regulations previously made under this subsection, saving and transitional provisions.

(3) The donor of an enduring power may in the document creating the power appoint one or more specified persons, being persons who are not disqualified, to act as attorney if an attorney appointed by the power dies or is unable or declines to act or is disqualified from acting as attorney.

(4) A power of attorney cannot be an enduring power unless, when executing the instrument creating it, the attorney is—

(a) (i) an individual who has attained 18 years and has not been adjudicated bankrupt or convicted of an offence involving fraud or dishonesty or an offence against the person or property of the donor or is not—

(I) a person in respect of whom a declaration has been made under section 150 of the Companies Act, 1990, or

(II) a person who is or was subject or deemed subject to a disqualification order by virtue of Part VII of that Act,

or

(ii) a trust corporation (within the meaning of section 30 of the Succession Act, 1965),

(b) not the owner of a nursing home (whether or not it is a nursing home within the meaning of the Health (Nursing Homes) Act, 1990) in which the donor resides, or a person residing with or an employee or agent of the owner, unless the attorney is a spouse, parent, child or sibling of the donor.

(5) A power of attorney which gives the attorney a right to appoint a substitute or successor cannot be an enduring power.

(6) Subject to subsection (8) and sections 14(3) and 14(5), an enduring power shall be invalidated or, as the case may be, shall cease to be in force on the adjudication in bankruptcy of the attorney or, if the attorney is a body corporate, by its winding up or dissolution or on the attorney being convicted of an offence referred to in subsection (4)(a)(i) or becoming—

(a) a person referred to in clause (I) or (II) of subsection (4)(a)(i), or

(b) an owner of a nursing home or other person referred to in subsection (4)(b),

unless the attorney is an attorney appointed by the power and subsection (3) applies.

(7) An enduring power in favour of a spouse shall, unless the power provides otherwise, be invalidated or, as the case may be, cease to be in force if subsequently—

(a) the marriage is either annulled under the law of the State or is annulled or dissolved under the law of another state and is, by reason of that annulment or divorce, not or no longer a subsisting valid marriage under the law of the State,

(b) either a decree of judicial separation is granted to either spouse by a court in the State or any decree is so granted by a court outside the State and is recognised in the State as having the like effect,

(c) a written agreement to separate is entered into between the spouses, or

(d) a protection order, interim barring order, barring order or safety order is made against the attorney on the application of the donor, or *vice versa*.

(8) Subsection (6) shall not apply to an enduring power which authorises, or to the extent that it authorises, an attorney to make personal care decisions on behalf of the donor unless the attorney has been convicted of an offence against the person of the donor or has become a person who would be disqualified from acting as attorney by virtue of subsection (4)(b).

(9) An enduring power shall be invalidated or, as the case may be, shall cease to be in force on the exercise by the court of any of its powers under the Lunacy Regulation (Ireland) Act, 1871, if the court so directs.

(10) No disclaimer, whether by deed or otherwise, of an enduring power which has not been registered under section 10 shall be valid unless and until the attorney gives notice of it to the donor.

(11) In subsection (4)(b) "owner" includes a person managing a nursing home or a director (including a shadow director within the meaning of section 27 of the Companies Act, 1990) of, or a shareholder in, a company which owns or manages such a home.

GENERAL NOTE

Section 5(1) states the kernel of an enduring power, which is that the donor intends it to be effective during his or her subsequent mental incapacity. (See definition of "mental incapacity".)

Subsection (2) empowers the Minister to make regulations in relation to certain matters concerning enduring powers. These regulations have been made and are embodied in Statutory Instruments Nos. 196 and 287 of 1996 (see Appendices A and B below, pp. 37 and 57). The regulations are quite technical and ought to be followed slavishly by practitioners. *Inter alia*, they provide for the form and execution of enduring powers. Section 10(5)(a) provides that the enduring power shall be treated as sufficient in point of form and expression if it differs in an immaterial respect from the form prescribed by the regulations. Furthermore, section 10(5)(b) provides that the court may, although the enduring power does not comply with the provisions of section 5 or regulations made thereunder, register the enduring power under certain circumstances. No practitioner will want to run the risk of having to make an application to the court (and presumably pay the costs thereof) because he or she was not careful enough in preparing the enduring power.

According to the Registrar of Wards of Court, common mistakes made in relation to the preparation and registration of Enduring Powers of Attorney include:
— Leaving out Part A of the Enduring Power, headed "Explanatory Memorandum". This is an integral part of the power.
— Not having proof of service of notices of execution of the Enduring Power available on an application for registration. Affidavits of Service of these Notices should be sworn immediately following service and kept with the original Power.

The Regulations provide for an Explanatory Memorandum, which forms part of the enduring power, to ensure that the latter incorporates adequate information as to the effect of creating or accepting the power.

It is interesting to note at this stage that the power has to be executed by four classes of people: the donor, a solicitor, a registered medical practitioner, and the attorney.

The making of the statement by the registered medical practitioner (that, in his or her opinion, at the time the document was executed the donor had mental capacity) was made slightly easier by the addition in the Act of the words "in his or her opinion" in section 5(2)(d)(iii).

The statement to be made by the attorney (that he or she understands the requirements of registration under section 10) was strengthened by the addition in the Act of the words "the duties and obligations of an attorney".

Subparagraphs (e) and (f) of section 5(2) had not been included in the Bill and were added to the Act to allay concerns that attorneys might not keep adequate accounts or might remunerate themselves in an uncontrolled way. The regulations provide that an attorney "shall keep adequate accounts of the management" of the property and affairs of the donor and "in particular, of any expenditure to meet the needs of persons other than the donor or to make any gifts authorised by the enduring power". The regulations also provide that the enduring power "may make provision in relation to the remuneration of an attorney". If no such provision is made, then the attorney can only recover out of pocket expenses.

The regulations provide that notice of the execution of the enduring power by the donor "shall be given by or on behalf of the donor to at least two persons named by the donor in the enduring power." None of them shall be an attorney under the power. At least one of them shall be:
1. the donor's spouse, if living with the donor; or
2. if clause (i) does not apply, a child of the donor: or
3. if clauses (i) and (ii) do not apply, a relative (if any) of the donor. The form of notice of execution is given in the regulations.

Subsection (3) was not in the Bill and was added to permit the appointment of substitute attorneys to act in the circumstances specified in the subsection.

As originally drafted in the Bill, subsection (4)(a)(i) simply referred to "an individual who has attained 18 years and is not a bankrupt". The additions were made in the interests of protecting a donor against a dishonest or oppressive attorney.

Subsection (4)(b) was supplemented by the substitution for the words "in the employment of" by the words "an employee or agent".

Subsection (6) provides for the invalidation of an enduring power when the circumstances mentioned therein arise, including the bankruptcy, winding up or dissolution of the attorney, or the attorney becoming an owner of a nursing home in which the donor resides.

Subsection (7) was widened, as a result of representations made after the publication of the Bill, by the addition of subparagraphs (c) and (d). Subsection (7) was amended by section 50 of the Family Law (Divorce) Act 1996 by the substitution of the following paragraph:

> "(a) The marriage is annulled or dissolved either—
> (i) Under the law of the State, or
> (ii) Under the law of another State and is, by reason of that annulment or divorce, not or no longer a subsisting valid marriage under the law of the State,".

Subsection (8) provides that the enduring power shall not be invalidated by reason of subsection (6) to the extent that it authorises the attorney to make personal care decisions, unless the attorney has been convicted of an offence against the person of the donor or has become disqualified by subsection (4)(b).

Subsection (10) refers to the disclaimer of enduring powers by their attorneys, providing that a disclaimer of an enduring power which has not been registered shall not be effective unless and until the attorney has given notice of disclaimer to the donor. After an enduring power has been registered it can only be disclaimed, on notice to the donor, with the consent of the court.

It should be noted that subsection (11) substantially widens the definition of "owner" of a nursing home.

Scope of authority of attorney under enduring power

6.—(1) An enduring power may confer general authority (as defined in subsection (2)) on the attorney to act on the donor's behalf in relation to all or a specified part of the property and affairs of the donor or may confer on the attorney authority to do specified things on the donor's behalf and the authority may, in either case, be conferred subject to conditions and restrictions.

(2) Where an instrument is expressed to confer general authority on the attorney, it operates to confer, subject to the restriction imposed by subsection (5) and to any conditions or restrictions contained in the instrument, authority to do on behalf of the donor anything which the donor can lawfully do by attorney.

(3) Subject to any conditions or restrictions contained in the instrument, an attorney under an enduring power, whether general or limited, may execute or exercise any of the powers or discretions vested in the donor as a tenant for life within the meaning of the Settled Land Act, 1882.

(4) Subject to any conditions or restrictions contained in the instrument, an attorney under an enduring power, whether general or limited, may act under the power for the attorney's benefit or that of other persons to the following extent but no further, that is to say, the attorney—

    (a) may so act in relation to himself or herself or in relation to any other person if the donor might be expected to provide for his or her or that person's needs respectively; and

    (b) may do whatever the donor might be expected to do to meet those needs.

(5) Without prejudice to subsection (4) but subject to any conditions or restrictions contained in the instrument, an attorney under an enduring power, whether general or limited, may, if specific provision to that effect is made in the instrument, dispose of the property of the donor by way of gift to the following extent but no further, that is to say, by making—

(a) gifts of a seasonal nature or at a time, or on an anniversary, of a birth or marriage, to persons (including the attorney) who are related to or connected with the donor, and

(b) gifts to any charity to which the donor made or might be expected to make gifts,

provided that the value of each such gift is not unreasonable having regard to all the circumstances and in particular the extent of the donor's assets.

(6) An enduring power may also confer authority on the attorney to make any specified personal care decision or decisions on the donor's behalf.

(7) (a) Any personal care decision made by an attorney on behalf of a donor shall be made in the donor's best interests.

(b) In deciding what is in a donor's best interests regard shall be had to the following:
   (i) so far as ascertainable, the past and present wishes and feelings of the donor and the factors which the donor would consider if he or she were able to do so;
   (ii) the need to permits and encourage the donor to participate, or to improve the donor's ability to participate, as fully as possible in any decision affecting the donor;
   (iii) so far as it is practicable and appropriate to consult any of the persons mentioned below, their views as to the donor's wishes and feelings and as to what would be in the donor's best interests:
      (I) any person named by the donor as someone to be consulted on those matters;
      (II) anyone (whether the donor's spouse, a relative, friend or other person) engaged in caring for the donor or interested in the donor's welfare;
   (iv) whether the purpose for which any decision is required can be as effectively achieved in a manner less restrictive of the donor's freedom of action.

(c) In the case of any personal care decision made by an attorney it shall be a sufficient compliance with paragraph (a) if the attorney reasonably believes that what he or she decides is in the best interests of the donor.

GENERAL NOTE

Section 6(1) provides that the enduring power can confer general authority on the attorney, or authority to do specified things on the donor's behalf. Subsection (2) defines "general authority" in a rather unhelpful way, providing that "general authority" is authority to do anything which the donor could lawfully do by attorney. At common law an attorney has no power to make gifts (*Re Bowles* (1874) 31 L.T. 365). Nor can an attorney make a will for the donor. However, see subsection (5) which gives the donee the power to make certain gifts in certain circumstances. While the basic rule is that an agent has no right to delegate, having decided on the course of action authorised by the power of attorney, an attorney has authority to employ, *e.g.* solicitors, auctioneers, accountants and so on, to implement that decision (see *Ex-parte Frampton; Re Frampton* (1859) 1 De G. & F.&J. 263, C.A.).

Section 6(3) specifically empowers an attorney under an enduring power to do whatever the donor could have done as a tenant for life under the Settled Land Act 1882 (see section (3) thereof).

Subsection (4) permits an attorney to act for the attorney's own benefit, or for the benefit of other persons, but only if the donor might be expected to provide for the attorney's or that other person's needs, and may only do whatever the donor might be expected to do to meet those needs. The power given to an attorney under subsection (4) is not, therefore, restricted to situations where the donor owes a family or moral duty to the attorney or the other person in question.

Subsection (5) further empowers the attorney, if the enduring power specifically so provides, to make gifts of the property of the donor of a seasonal nature, or at certain times or anniversaries, to people (including the attorney) who are related to or connected with the donor, and gifts to any charity to which the donor made or might be expected to make gifts. The only restriction here is that the value of each gift is not to be unreasonable having regard to all the circumstances and to the extent of the donor's assets. Once again it should be noted that this subsection is quite wide, and authorises certain gifts not only to relations, but also to people who are "connected with" the donor. Paragraph 5 of the regulations (S.I. No. 196 of 1996) made under section 5 imposes a duty on the attorney to keep a record of any such gifts. It could be argued that an attorney should have been empowered by the Act to make gifts outside of the restrictions imposed by subsection (5), in the context, for example, of inheritance tax planning. However, it would appear that the subsection as drafted does not go as far as to authorise this.

Subsection (6) was an innovation, not having been included in the original Bill. "Personal care decisions" are defined in section 4. It is possible to make one enduring power conferring on a certain attorney the power to make personal care decisions, and a second enduring power conferring on a different attorney the power to make decisions relating to the "affairs" of the donor.

Subsection (7) provides that the personal care decision must be made in the donor's best interests and states that regard must be had to certain circumstances in deciding what is in the donor's best interests. It further provides that certain people must be consulted in relation to the donor's wishes and feelings, and his or her best interests. However, the last word is clearly given to the attorney by subparagraph (c) of subsection (7).

The Act is silent as to whether the donee of an enduring power can continue administering the estate of a deceased person of which the donor, who has lost mental capacity, is personal representative. In England, if the donor of an enduring or ordinary power of attorney is entitled to apply for a grant of probate or letters of administration, his or her attorney can apply for administration for the use and benefit of the donor under rule 31(1) of the (English) Non-Contentious Probate Rules 1987 (S.I. No. 2024 of 1987) provided he has authority to do so under the power – a general power gives such authority. The grant may be limited until further representation be granted, or in such other way as the Registrar may direct. Given that under Irish law a grant of representation may be made to the attorney of the person entitled (Rules of the Superior Courts 1986 (S.I. No. 15 of 1986) Order 79, rule 23) there seems to be no substantive reason why a grant of representation cannot be made to the donee of an enduring power who is entitled to the grant.

Coming into force and survival of enduring power

7.—(1) Where an individual creates an enduring power of attorney—
    (a) subject to subsection (2) and section 9, the power shall not come into force until it has been registered under section 10; and
    (b) the power shall not be revoked by the donor's subsequent mental incapacity.

(2) Where the attorney has made an application for registration of the instrument then, until the application has been determined, the attorney may take action under the power—
    (a) to maintain the donor or prevent loss to the donor's estate,
    (b) to maintain the attorney or other persons in so far as that is permitted under section 6(4), or

(c) to make a personal care decision which cannot reasonably be deferred until the application has been determined.

(3) Where the attorney purports to act as provided by subsection (2) then, in favour of a person who deals with the attorney without knowledge that the attorney is acting otherwise than in accordance with that subsection, the transaction between them shall be as valid as if the attorney were acting in accordance therewith.

GENERAL NOTE

Section 7(1) provides that the enduring power shall not come into force until it has been registered, subject to subsection (2) and "section 9". One wonders if the reference to "section 9" here should have been a reference to "section 8", and it was indeed so referred to in the Bill (see below).

Subsection (2) provides that where the attorney has applied for registration he or she may act under the power to do certain important things, including maintaining the donor, preventing loss to the donor's assets, and making personal care decisions which cannot reasonably be deferred. Bona fide third parties who deal with the attorney who is acting under subsection (2) are protected by subsection (3).

Functions of court prior to registration

8.—Where the court has reason to believe that the donor of an enduring power may be, or may be becoming, mentally incapable and the court is of the opinion that it is necessary, before the instrument creating the power is registered, to exercise any power with respect to the power of attorney or the attorney appointed to act under it which would become exercisable under section 12 on its registration, the court may on application to it by any interested party exercise that power under this section and may do so whether the attorney has or has not made an application to the court for the registration of the instrument.

GENERAL NOTE

Section 8 permits the court to exercise an enduring power on application to the court by any interested party, where the donor may, or may be becoming, mentally incapable and the court is of the opinion that it is necessary to exercise a power under the enduring power. This may be the case if the attorney has, or even if the attorney has not, applied to the court for the registration of the enduring power. This would, for example, apply to a situation where the donor was becoming mentally incapable but the attorney could not be easily contacted.

Application for registration

9.—(1) If the attorney under an enduring power has reason to believe that the donor is or is becoming mentally incapable, the attorney shall, as soon as practicable, make an application to the court for the registration of the instrument creating the power.

(2) Before making the application the attorney shall comply with the provisions as to notice set out in the First Schedule.

(3) The attorney may, before making the application, refer to the court for its determination any question as to the validity of the power.

(4) A certificate to the effect that the donor is, or is becoming, incapable by reason of a mental condition of managing and administering his or her own

property and affairs and purporting to be signed by a registered medical practitioner may be accepted as evidence of the matters contained therein.

(5) Any person who, in an application for registration, makes a statement which he or she knows to be false in a material particular shall be liable—
- (a) on conviction on indictment, to imprisonment for a term not exceeding two years or to a fine not exceeding £10,000, or both; and
- (b) on summary conviction, to imprisonment for a term not exceeding six months or to a fine not exceeding £1,000, or both.

(6) Pending the making of other provision by rules of court an application under subsection (1) shall be addressed to the Registrar of Wards of Court.

GENERAL NOTE

Section 9 is vital in that it imposes an obligation on the attorney to apply to the court for the registration of the power once the attorney has reason to believe that the donor is or is becoming mentally incapable. Before making the application the attorney must give the notice referred to in the First Schedule. Interestingly, section 5 did not empower the Minister to make regulations concerning the form of the certificate to be given by the registered medical practitioner under subsection (4) that the donor is or is becoming incapable by reason of a mental condition of managing and administering his or her own property and affairs. This certificate is clearly indispensable to the application for registration. Subsection (4) did not appear in the Bill as originally drafted.

Subsection (6) provides for the application for registration under subsection (1) to be "addressed to the Registrar of Wards of Court". The original procedure for applying for registration was laid down in the Practice Direction, reproduced in Appendix C (pp. 61–63). This procedure was quite complicated, involving, for example, the issue of a Special Summons. The Rules of Court (S.I. No. 66 of 2000), reproduced in Appendix D (pp. 65–69) provide for a simpler application for registration to be made to the Registrar of Wards of Court.

Registration

10.—(1) On an application for registration being made in compliance with section 9 the Registrar of Wards of Court shall, unless subsection (2) applies, register the instrument to which the application relates.

(2) If, in the case of an application for registration—
- (a) a valid notice of objection to the registration pursuant to subsection (3) from a person to whom an attorney has given notice pursuant to paragraph 2(1) of the First Schedule is received by the court before the expiry of the period of five weeks beginning with the date on which that notice was given,
- (b) it appears from the application that there is no one to whom notice has been given under paragraph 2 of that Schedule, or
- (c) there is reason to believe that appropriate enquiries might bring to light evidence on which the court could be satisfied that one of the grounds of objection set out in subsection (3) was established,

the court shall neither register the instrument nor refuse the application until it has made or caused to be made such enquiries (if any) as it thinks appropriate in the circumstances of the case.

(3) For the purposes of this Act a notice of objection to the registration of an instrument is valid if the objection is made on one or more of the following

grounds, namely—
- (a) that the power purported to have been created by the instrument was not valid;
- (b) that the power created by the instrument is no longer a valid and subsisting power;
- (c) that the donor is not or is not becoming mentally incapable;
- (d) that, having regard to all the circumstances, the attorney is unsuitable to be the donor's attorney;
- (e) that fraud or undue pressure was used to induce the donor to create the power.

(4) The court may refuse the application on any of the grounds of objection set out in subsection (3).

(5) (a) Where an instrument differs in an immaterial respect in form or mode of expression from the form prescribed by regulations under section 5(2)(a) the instrument shall be treated as sufficient in point of form and expression.

(b) The court may, notwithstanding that an instrument may not comply with the provisions of section 5 or regulations made thereunder, register the instrument as an enduring power if it is satisfied—
- (i) that the donor intended the power to be effective during any mental incapacity of the donor,
- (ii) that the power was not executed as a result of any fraud or undue pressure,
- (iii) that the attorney is suitable to be the donor's attorney, and
- (iv) that it is desirable in the interests of justice so to register the instrument.

(6) Where at the time of the application for registration there is in force under the Lunacy Regulation (Ireland) Act, 1871, an order appointing a committee of the estate of the donor but the power created by the instrument has not also been revoked, the court shall make such order as seems to it proper in the circumstances including, if appropriate, an order revoking the order already made under the said Act.

GENERAL NOTE

Section 10(1) provides that the Registrar of Wards of Court shall register the enduring power unless subsection (2) applies.

Subsection (2)(a) applies where a valid notice of objection to the registration of the enduring power has been received from a party to whom notice has been given under paragraph 2(1) of the First Schedule (below). Subsection (2)(b) applies where notice has not been given under paragraph 3 of Part I of the First Schedule (see below). Subsection (2)(c) applies where the Registrar of Wards of Court has reason to believe that one of the grounds of objection set out in paragraph 3 could be established.

Subsection (2) goes on to state that "the court" (meaning the High Court) shall then neither register the enduring power nor refuse the application for registration until it has made appropriate enquiries. Presumably what is intended is that if the Registrar of Wards of Court believes that subsection (2) applies he or she will inform a judge of the High Court accordingly, and await a decision of the court as to whether the enduring power should or should not be registered.

Subsection (4) provides that the court may refuse the application for registration of the enduring power on any of the grounds of objection set out in subsection (3). The Practice

Direction (reproduced in Appendix C, p. 61) stated that where subsection (2) applies the Registrar shall obtain the directions of the President of the High Court or a judge nominated by him or her as to what enquiries are to be made, what persons should be given notice of the hearing, the date of the hearing and any other matter required to enable the court to exercise its jurisdiction under the Act. This is now referred to in Rule 3(5) of S.I. 66 of 2000 (reproduced in Appendix D).

In the only reported case on the provisions of the Act to date, Morris P. in *Re Hamilton's Application* [1999] 2 I.L.R.M. 509 considered an objection to the registration of an enduring power on the basis that the proposed Attorneys were not suitable persons within the meaning of section 10 because of the manner in which, it was alleged, they had mismanaged the donor's affairs to the date of the execution of the enduring power. Morris P. held that the complaints of mismanagement were misdirected because at the time of the matters complained of the donor was capable of, and was managing, her affairs. Thus, even if the criticisms were valid, they were not validly made of and concerning the proposed attorneys.

Morris P. also held that the word "unsuitable" as used in section 10 does not pertain to the proposed attorney's skill at managing the donor's property and it would be an improper exercise of the discretion vested in the Court to refuse to register the power because the chosen attorney did not possess a high degree of management and business skills. The grounds of objection set out in section 10 are fundamental in nature, and for an objection to succeed, a criticism far more fundamental than mere lack of management skills would have to be established. A criticism made of a proposed attorney, to constitute a ground for refusing to register the power, "must far exceed the corresponding test applied by the courts in applications for the removal of a trustee".

Subsection (3) provides for valid grounds of objection to the registration of the enduring power. It should be noted that registration cannot take place within five weeks from the date notice has been given pursuant to paragraph 2(1) of the First Schedule. Subsection (5) did not appear in the original Bill and is important because it permits an enduring power to be treated as sufficient "in point of form and expression", even though it differs in an immaterial respect from the form prescribed by regulations. Furthermore even if the enduring power does not comply with the provisions of section 5, or the regulations made thereunder, the court may still register it if it is satisfied with all of the four requirements specified in subsection (5)(b).

Subsection (5)(b) has been interpreted to permit the registration of an enduring power executed in accordance with English law provided satisfactory affidavit evidence is available to satisfy the requirements of the subsection.

Subsection (6) provides that where a committee has been appointed under the Lunacy Regulation (Ireland) Act 1871, but the enduring power has not also been revoked, the court may make such order as it deems appropriate, including an order revoking the order already made under the said Act.

Effect and proof of registration

11.—(1) The effect of the registration of an instrument is that—
  (a) no revocation of the power by the donor shall be valid unless and until the court confirms the revocation under section 12(3);
  (b) no disclaimer of the power shall be valid except on notice to the donor and with the consent of the court;
  (c) the donor may not extend or restrict the scope of the authority conferred by the instrument and no consent or instruction given by the donor after registration shall, in the case of a consent, confer any right and, in the case of an instruction, impose or confer any obligation or right on or create any liability of the attorney or other persons having notice of the consent or instruction.

(2) Subsection (1) applies for so long as the instrument is registered whether

or not the donor is for the time being mentally capable.

(3) On registration of an enduring power the Registrar of Wards of Court shall supply an attested copy of the enduring power to the donor and any persons who were given notice under paragraph 2 of the First Schedule of the application for registration.

(4) Members of the public may inspect the register free of charge during normal office hours.

(5) A document purporting to be a copy, attested by an officer of the Office of Wards of Court, of an instrument registered under this Act shall be evidence of the contents of the instrument and of the fact that it has been so registered.

(6) Subsection (5) is without prejudice to section 21 (proof by certified copies) and to any other method of proof authorised by law.

GENERAL NOTE

Section 11 set out the effects of the registration of the enduring power:
1. After registration, the power cannot be revoked by the donor without the consent of the court. (Although there is no specific provision as to the form of revocation of a power of attorney, it is clear that an enduring power may be revoked prior to registration. It would be prudent for the donor, in such circumstances, to give notice of revocation to the donee, to the parties to give notice of the execution of the power had been given, and to any financial institutions with which the donor has dealt. It is frequently the case that the donor has given both an ordinary and an enduring power to the same person. If one is revoked then clearly the other should be revoked simultaneously.)
2. The attorney cannot disclaim the power without the consent of the High Court.
3. The donor may not extend or restrict the authority conferred by the power.

Subsection (2) provides that the effects of registration of the power shall apply only for as long as the enduring power is registered, whether or not the donor is mentally incapable.

Functions of court with respect to registered power

12.—(1) Where an instrument has been registered the court shall, on application to it by the donor, the attorney or any other interested party, as the case may be, have the functions set out in subsections (2) to (6).

(2) The court may—
    (a) determine any question as to the meaning or effect of the instrument;
    (b) give directions with respect to—
        (i) the management or disposal by the attorney of the property and affairs of the donor;
        (ii) the rendering of accounts by the attorney and the production of the records kept by the attorney for that purpose;
        (iii) the remuneration or expenses of the attorney, whether or not in default of or in accordance with any provision made by the instrument, including directions for the repayment of excessive, or the payment of additional, remuneration;
        (iv) a personal care decision made or to be made by the attorney;
    (c) require the attorney to furnish information or produce documents or things in his or her possession as attorney;
    (d) give any consent or authorisation to act which the attorney would have to obtain from a mentally capable donor;
    (e) authorise the attorney to act for the attorney's own benefit or that of

other persons than the donor otherwise than in accordance with section 6(4) and (5) (but subject to any conditions or restrictions contained in the instrument);

(f) where appropriate, relieve the attorney wholly or partly from any liability incurred or which may have been incurred on account of a breach of duty as attorney.

(3) On application on notice to the attorney made for the purpose by or on behalf of the donor, the court shall confirm the revocation of the power if satisfied that the donor has done whatever is necessary in law to effect an express revocation of the power and was mentally capable of revoking a power of attorney at the time of the purported revocation.

(4) The court may cancel the registration of an instrument in any of the following circumstances, that is to say—

(a) on confirming the revocation of the power under subsection (3) or consenting to a disclaimer under section 11(1)(b);

(b) on giving a direction revoking the power on exercising any of its powers under the Lunacy Regulation (Ireland) Act, 1871;

(c) on being satisfied that the donor is and is likely to remain mentally capable;

(d) on being satisfied that the power has ceased to be in force by the death or adjudication in bankruptcy of the donor or by virtue of subsection (7) or (9) of section 5 or by the death or mental incapacity of the attorney or by virtue of section 5(6);

(e) on being satisfied that the power was not a valid and subsisting enduring power when registration was effected;

(f) on being satisfied that, having regard to all the circumstances, the attorney is unsuitable to be the donor's attorney;

(g) on being satisfied that fraud or undue pressure was used to induce the donor to create the power; or

(h) for any other good and sufficient reason.

(5) Where the court cancels the registration of an instrument on being satisfied of the matters specified in paragraph (f) or (g) of subsection (4) it shall by order revoke the power created by the instrument.

(6) On the cancellation of the registration of an instrument under subsection (4) (other than paragraph (c)) the instrument shall be delivered up to be cancelled, unless the court otherwise directs.

GENERAL NOTE

Section 12 sets out the functions of the court, after the enduring power has been registered, where application is made to the court by the donor, the attorney, or "any other interested party".

It should be noted that subsection (2)(e) permits a court to extend the provisions of section 6(4) and (5), which apply to provision for the needs of the attorney or any other person the donor might be expected to provide for, and certain types of gifts.

Subsection (3) empowers the court to confirm the revocation of the enduring power on the application of the donor in a situation where the donor is mentally capable of revoking the power.

Subsection (4) sets out the court's powers to cancel the registration of an enduring power. These powers are wide and include the power to cancel the registration of an enduring power "for any other good and sufficient reason". Subsection (4)(h) did not appear in the original Bill.

Subsection (5) provides that where the court cancels the registration of the power on the grounds of the unsuitability of the attorney or for fraud or undue pressure, the court shall revoke the enduring power also.

Subsection (6) provides that when the registration of the enduring power is cancelled, the instrument creating the enduring power shall be delivered up to be cancelled, except in the circumstances where the donor is and is likely to remain mentally capable. There is an implication here that if the donor became mentally incapable again, an enduring power could be re-registered.

Protection of attorney and third person where registered power invalid or not in force

13.—(1) Subsections (2) and (3) apply where an instrument which did not create a valid enduring power has been registered, whether or not the registration has been cancelled at the time of the act or transaction in question.

(2) An attorney who acts in pursuance of an enduring power which is not or no longer a valid power or which has ceased to be in force shall not thereby incur any liability (either to the donor or to any other person) unless at the time of acting the attorney knows—
  (a) that the instrument did not create a valid enduring power; or
  (b) that an event has occurred which, if the instrument had recreated a valid enduring power, would have invalidated the power or caused it to cease to be in force; or
  (c) that the instrument has been cancelled.

(3) Any transaction between the attorney and another person shall, in favour of that person, be as valid as if the power had then been in existence, unless at the time of the transaction that person has knowledge of any of the matters mentioned in subsection (2).

(4) Where the interest of a purchaser depends on whether a transaction between the attorney and another person was valid by virtue of subsection (3), it shall be presumed in favour of the purchaser unless the contrary is shown that the transaction was valid if—
  (a) the transaction between that person and the attorney was completed within twelve months of the date on which the instrument was registered; or
  (b) that person makes a statutory declaration, before or within three months after the completion of the purchase, that he or she had no reason at the time of the transaction to doubt that the attorney had authority to dispose of the property which was the subject of the transaction.

(5) For the purposes of section 18 (protection of attorney and third persons where action is taken under the power of attorney in ignorance of its having been revoked) in its application to an enduring power the revocation of which by the donor is by virtue of section 11(1)(a) invalid unless and until confirmed by the court under section 12(3), knowledge of the confirmation of the revocation is, but knowledge of the unconfirmed revocation is not, knowledge of the revocation of the power.

(6) In this section "purchaser" has the meaning assigned to it by section 18(6) and "purchase" shall be construed accordingly.

GENERAL NOTE

Section 13(2) and (3) protect attorneys and third persons who have acted in reliance on the validity of an enduring power, unless they knew the instrument did not create a valid enduring power, that an event has occurred which would have caused the power to cease to be in force, or that the instrument creating the power has been cancelled. The question arises as to whether those relying on the protection of subsections (2) and (3) check with the register of enduring powers of attorney, or can they rely on section 11(5) which provides that a document purporting to be a copy, attested by an officer of the Office of Wards of Court, of an instrument registered under the Act, shall be evidence of the contents of the instrument and of the fact that it has been so registered?

While section 12(6) provides that when an instrument creating a power is cancelled, the instrument shall be delivered up to be cancelled, what if an official copy is still in existence after the cancellation of the instrument? It would, presumably, always be prudent practice to check the Register of Enduring Powers of Attorney.

Subsection (4) provides that it shall be presumed in favour of a purchaser whose interest depends on whether a transaction between the attorney and another person is valid by virtue of subsection (3) that the transaction was valid:
– if the transaction between that person and the attorney was completed within 12 months of the date of registration of the enduring power, or
– if that person makes the statutory declaration referred to in subsection (4)(b).

"Purchaser" is defined in section 18(6). The purchaser must be in good faith and must acquire an interest in property for valuable consideration. Thus, the person who deals directly with the attorney is protected by section 13(3), and the purchaser who deals with that person is protected by section 13(4) provided the provisions of subparagraphs (a) and (b) of subsection (4) are complied with. A duty is here imposed on conveyancers to ensure compliance with subsection (4) where they are acting for someone acquiring property from an attorney, as otherwise they may have difficulties when that person is disposing of the property later.

Subsection (5) helpfully provides that knowledge of the confirmation of the revocation of an enduring power is not knowledge for the purposes of section 18 (see below, p. 24) unless the revocation of the power has been confirmed by the court.

Application to joint and joint and several attorneys

14.—(1) An instrument which appoints more than one person to be an attorney may specify that the attorneys are appointed to act either jointly or jointly and severally. In default, the attorneys shall be deemed to have been appointed to act jointly.

(2) This Act, in its application to joint attorneys, applies to them collectively as it applies to a single attorney but subject to the modifications specified in subsection (3) and Part I of the Second Schedule.

(3) Where two or more persons are appointed (or are deemed to have been appointed) to act jointly, then, in the case of the death, incapacity or disqualification of any one or more of them, the remaining attorney or attorneys may continue to act, whether solely or jointly as the case may be, unless the instrument creating the power expressly provides to the contrary.

(4) This Act, in its application to joint and several attorneys, applies with the modifications specified in subsections (5) to (8) and in Part II of the Second Schedule.

(5) A failure, as respects any other attorney, to comply with the provisions of section 5 and regulations made thereunder shall prevent the instrument from applying in that attorney's case without however affecting its efficacy as respects the other or others.

(6) Where one or more but not both or all the attorneys makes or joins in making an application for registration of the instrument then—
  (a) an attorney who is not an applicant as well as one who is may act pending the determination of the application as provided in section 7(2) (or under section 8);
  (b) notice of the application shall also be given under the First Schedule to the other attorney or attorneys; and
  (c) objection may validly be taken to the registration on a ground relating to an attorney or to the power of an attorney who is not an applicant as well as to one or the power of one who is an applicant.

(7) The court shall not refuse under section 10(4) to register an instrument because a ground of objection to an attorney or a power is established if an enduring power subsists as respects an attorney who is not affected thereby but shall give effect to it by the prescribed qualification of the registration.

(8) The court shall not cancel the registration of an instrument under section 12(4) in any of the circumstances specified in that subsection if an enduring power subsists as respects an attorney who is not affected thereby but shall give effect to it by the prescribed qualification of the registration.

(9) In this section—

"prescribed" means prescribed by rules of court; and

"the requirements for the creation of enduring powers" means the provisions of section 5 other than subsections (5) to (10) and of regulations under subsection (2) of that section.

GENERAL NOTE

In the First Schedule, Part A: Explanatory Memorandum, to the Enduring Powers of Attorney Regulations 1996 (S.I. No. 196 of 1996), it is stated that where the attorneys are appointed jointly they must all act together and cannot act separately; but when they are appointed jointly and severally they can all act together but they can also act separately if they wish. If the enduring power does not specify how the attorneys are to act, they shall be deemed to have been appointed to act jointly. If they are appointed or deemed to have been appointed to act jointly then under section 14(3) where one of them dies the remaining attorney or attorneys may continue to act, unless the instrument creating the power expressly provides to the contrary.

Subsection (5) makes it clear that where attorneys are appointed jointly and severally, the failure of one of the attorneys to comply with section 5 of the Act and regulations made thereunder shall not affect the efficacy of the power as respects the other attorney or attorneys. This would not be the case where the appointment was a joint one, because in that circumstance the attorneys must act together and, clearly, if one was failing to comply with section 5 or the regulations, the other or others could not act validly.

Subsection (6) refers to a situation where one or more, but not both or all of attorneys who are appointed jointly and severally applies for the registration of the instrument creating the power.

Subsection (7) deals with the situation where a ground of objection is established to an attorney, or a power, if the enduring power subsists as regards an attorney who is not thereby affected. Thus a power could be registered to the exclusion of one or more joint and several attorneys, if no objection is established to a surviving attorney or attorneys. Subsection (8) applies similar considerations to applications for the cancellation of a power.

Part III
Powers of Attorney Generally

GENERAL NOTE

This Part of the Act deals with powers of attorney generally, and some of its provisions would therefore also apply to enduring powers. The law concerning powers of attorney generally, until the passing of the Powers of Attorney Act 1996, was embodied in the common law and certain provisions of the Conveyancing Acts 1881 and 1882. Some provisions of these Acts are repealed by the Powers of Attorney Act 1996 (see General Note to section 25 below, p. 31).

Creation of power

15.—(1) Where an instrument creating a power of attorney is signed by direction of the donor it shall be signed in the presence of the donor and of another person who shall attest the instrument as witness.

(2) A power of attorney is not required to be made under seal.

(3) This section is without prejudice to any requirement in or under any other enactment as to the witnessing of powers of attorney or as to the execution of instruments by bodies corporate.

GENERAL NOTE

Section 15(1) refers to an instrument creating a power of attorney being signed by direction of the donor, presumably in circumstances where the donor is physically (but obviously not mentally) incapable of signing. Subsection (2) dispenses with the requirement that a power of attorney should be under seal (see General Note to section 2, above, p. 4). Subsection (3) contains a saver for any other statutory requirements for witnessing powers of attorney and for the rules governing the execution of instruments by bodies corporate.

Effect of general power in specified form

16.—(1) A general power of attorney in the form set out in the Third Schedule, or in a form to the like effect expressed to be made under this Act, shall operate to confer on the donee or donees of the power acting in accordance with its terms authority to do on behalf of the donor anything which the donor can lawfully do by attorney.

(2) This section does not apply to functions which the donor has as a trustee or personal representative or as a tenant for life within the meaning of the Settled Land Act, 1882, or as a trustee or other person exercising the powers of a tenant for life under section 60 of that Act.

GENERAL NOTE

Section 16 provides for the creation of a form (set out in the Third Schedule, p. 36) of general power of attorney which operates in the widest fashion, empowering the donee to do anything which the donor could lawfully do by attorney. The form will give practitioners the option of offering their clients a very simple form of general power of attorney. Subsection (2) makes it clear that this general form of power cannot be used to delegate the functions of a trustee, a personal representative, a tenant for life within the meaning of that term in the Settled Land Act 1882, or a trustee or other person exercising the powers of a tenant for life under section 60 of that Act.

Execution of instruments, etc. by donee of power

17.—(1) The donee of a power of attorney may—
   (a) execute any instrument with his or her own signature and, where sealing is required, with his or her own seal, and
   (b) do any other thing in his or her own name,

by the authority of the donor of the power; and any instrument executed or thing done in that manner shall be as effective as if executed or done by the donee with the signature and seal, or, as the case may be, in the name, of the donor of the power.

(2) A person who is authorised under a power of attorney to convey any estate or interest in property in the name or on behalf of a corporation sole or aggregate may either execute the conveyance as provided in subsection (1) or, as donee of the power, execute the conveyance by signing his or her name as acting in the name or on behalf of the corporation in the presence of at least one witness and, in the case of a deed, by affixing his or her own seal, and such execution takes effect and is valid in like manner as if the corporation had executed the conveyance.

(3) Where a corporation aggregate is authorised under a power of attorney to convey any interest in property in the name or on behalf of any other person (including another body corporate), a person appointed for that purpose by the corporation may execute the deed or other instrument in the name of such other person; and where an instrument appears to be executed by a person so appointed then in favour of a purchaser the instrument is deemed to have been executed by that person, unless the contrary is shown.

(4) In this section "purchaser" has the meaning given to it by section 18(6).

(5) This section applies whenever the power of attorney was created.

GENERAL NOTE

Section 17(1) re-enacts section 46 of the Conveyancing Act 1881 which authorised a donee of power to execute or do any assurance, instrument or thing in and with his or her own name, signature and seal (where sealing is required) by the authority of the donor. Section 46 of the Conveyancing Act 1881 related solely to the execution of deeds by an attorney. Section 17(1) of the 1996 Act provides that the donee of a power of attorney may execute any instrument or do any other thing either in his or her own name (with his or her own signature or seal where appropriate) and by the authority of the donor, or in the name of the donor. Where a company is acting as attorney, any individual appointed for that purpose by the company may execute a deed or other instrument in the name of the donor. Such execution will be valid in favour of a purchaser where the instrument indicated that the person executing it had such authority, unless the contrary is shown.

Section 17(2) provides that were a power of attorney is being exercised on behalf of a corporation, the donee may execute a conveyance "by signing his or her own name as acting in the name or on behalf of the corporation in the presence of at least one witness and, in the case of a deed, by affixing his or her own seal". Although the general provision in subsection (1) applies, it would be prudent for this special method of execution to be used whenever a conveyance of property is made by an attorney on behalf of a corporation.

The best practice in relation to the execution of deeds by the donee of a power of attorney is as follows:
1. the deed is prepared in the name of the donor;
2. the attestation clause states that the deed is executed on behalf of the donor by the attorney;
3. the donee executes by writing in his or her own hand "AB (the donor) by his or her

attorney CD (the donee)" who then signs his or her own name.

Subsection (3) authorises bodies aggregate, when donees of powers of attorney, to appoint persons to execute a deed to convey any interest in property in the name of the donor of a power. Subsection (4) gives the meaning to "purchaser" that is given by section 18(6).

Subsection (5) applies section 17 to powers of attorney executed either before or after the coming into operation of the Powers of Attorney Act 1996. Presumably this subsection therefore corrects any invalidity in the execution by a donee of a power in the sense that a form of execution which may have been invalid prior to the August 1, 1996, may be valid thereafter.

Protection of donee and other persons where power revoked

18.—(1) A donee of a power of attorney who acts in pursuance of the power at a time when it has been revoked shall not, by reason of the revocation, incur any liability (either to the donor or to any other person) if at that time the donee did not know that the power had been revoked.

(2) Where a power of attorney has been revoked and a person, without knowledge of the revocation, deals with the donee of the power, the transaction between them shall, in favour of that person, be as valid as if the power had then been in force.

(3) Where the power is expressed in the instrument creating it to be irrevocable and to be given by way of security then, unless the person dealing with the donee knows that it was not in fact given by way of security, that person shall be entitled to assume that the power is incapable of revocation except by the donor acting with the consent of the donee and shall accordingly be treated for the purposes of subsection (2) as having knowledge of the revocation only if that person knows that it has been revoked in that manner.

(4) Where the interest of a purchaser depends on whether a transaction between the donee of a power of attorney and another person was valid by virtue of subsection (2), it shall be presumed in favour of the purchaser unless the contrary is shown that that person did not at the material time know of the revocation of the power if—

 (a) the transaction between that person and the donee was completed within twelve months of the date on which the power came into operation, or
 (b) that person makes a statutory declaration, before or within three months after the completion of the purchase, that that person did not at the material time know of the revocation of the power.

(5) Without prejudice to subsection (3), for the purposes of this section knowledge of the revocation of a power of attorney includes knowledge of the occurrence of any event (such as the death of the donor) which has the effect of revoking the power.

(6) In this section "purchaser" means a purchaser in good faith for valuable consideration and includes a lessee, mortgagee or other person who, for valuable consideration, acquires an interest in any property; and includes also an intending purchaser.

(7) This section applies to a power of attorney whenever created but only to acts and transactions after the commencement of this section.

Powers of Attorney Act 1996

GENERAL NOTE

Section 18 applies both to enduring powers and to ordinary powers of attorney, but in its application to enduring powers, practitioners should refer back to section 13(5). Section 18 replaces sections 8 and 9 of the Conveyancing Act 1882 and relates to the protection of the donee of a power of attorney and third parties where the power is revoked.

Section 8(1) of the Conveyancing Act 1882 provides:

"If a power of attorney, given for valuable consideration, is in the instrument creating the power expressed to be irrevocable, then, in favour of a purchaser,—
 (i) The power shall not be revoked at any time, either by anything done by the donor of the power without the concurrence of the donee of the power, or by the death, marriage, lunacy, unsoundness of mind or bankruptcy of the donor of the power; and
 (ii) Any Act done at any time by the donee of the power, in pursuance of the power, shall be as valid as if anything done by the donor of the power without the concurrence of the donee of the power, or the death, marriage, lunacy, unsoundness of mind, or bankruptcy of the donor of the power had not been done or happened; and
 (iii) Neither the donee of the power nor the purchaser shall at any time be prejudicially affected by notice of anything done by the donor of the power without he concurrence of the donee of the power, or of the death, marriage, lunacy, unsoundness of mind or bankruptcy of the donor of the power.
(2) This section applies only to powers of attorney created by instruments executed after the commencement of this Act".

Section 8 of the 1882 Act applied only to powers of attorney given for valuable consideration, which are expressed in the instrument creating the power to be irrevocable (see Wylie, *Irish Land Law* (2nd ed., 1997) paragraphs 11.37 to 11.39).

Section 9 of the Conveyancing Act 1882 provides:

"(1) If a power of attorney, whether given for valuable consideration or not, is in the instrument creating the power expressed to be irrevocable for a fixed time therein specified, not exceeding one year from the date of the instrument, then, in favour of a purchaser,—
 (i) The power shall not be revoked, for and during that fixed time, either by anything done by the donor of the power without the concurrence of the donee of the power, or by the death, marriage, lunacy, unsoundness of mind or bankruptcy of the donor of the power; and
 (ii) Any act donees in that fixed time, the donee of the power, in pursuance of the power, shall be as valid as if anything done by the donor of the power without the concurrence of the donee of the power, or the death, marriage, lunacy, unsoundness of mind, or bankruptcy of the donor that the power had not been done or happened; and
 (iii) Neither the donee of the power, nor the purchaser, shall at any time prejudicially affected by notice either during or after that fixed time of anything done by the donor of the power during that fixed time, without the concurrence of the donee of the power, or of the death, marriage, lunacy, unsoundness of mind, or bankruptcy of the donor of the power within that fixed time.
(2) This section applies only to powers of attorney created by instruments executed after the commencement of this Act."

The protection afforded by these sections to donees and purchasers where the power of attorney has been revoked was removed by the 1996 Act and replaced by the protection given by section 18 of that Act.

It should be noted, of course, that an enduring power cannot be revoked after registration without the confirmation of the court (see section 12(3) and (4)(a)). An enduring power may be revoked prior to registration, but this revocation can be of no significance to donees or purchasers because enduring power cannot come into force until it has been registered under section 10.

Section 7(2) of the 1996 Act does empower an attorney who has made an application for registration, until the application has been determined, to take action to, *inter alia*, maintain the donor or prevent loss to the donor's estate. Section 7(3) protects a person who deals with the attorney "without knowledge that the attorney is acting otherwise than in accordance with that subsection" where the attorney purports to act as provided by of section 7(2). The transaction between the attorney and such person shall be as valid as if the attorney were acting in accordance with 7(2).

At common law, a power of attorney was a "revokable instrument" (see *Bromley v. Holland* (1802) 7 Ves 3) and so the donor can revoke at any time unless it is an irrevocable power. It appears that the revocation can be oral, in writing or by deed (see *Re "The Margaret Mitchell"* (1888 Swab 382, 166 E.R. 174), but it is ineffective until it is received by the donee (see *Re Oriental Bank Corporation, ex-parte Guillemin* (1884) 28 Ch.D. 634). It appears that notice to one joint attorney is effective (see *Bristow and Porter v. Taylor* (1817) 2 Stark 50, 171 E.R. 568).

There would be no benefit in making an enduring power irrevocable, because an application can always be made to the court, after registration, to confirm revocation, and the enduring power cannot be used prior to registration except in the limited context of section 7.

Prior to the implementation of the 1996 Act, in relation to an ordinary power which is expressed to be irrevocable, donees and purchasers only had protection where the period of irrevocability did not exceed one year (see section 9 of the Conveyancing Act 1882, as quoted above). Apart from the case of the power given on security (see section 20, below, p. 27) there is now no benefit in making an ordinary power irrevocable, as the protection given by section 18 to donees and persons dealing with the donee applies whether or not the power is expressed to be irrevocable.

Section 18(1) deals with the protection of a donee who acts in pursuance of a power at a time when it has been revoked, if he or she did not know at that time that it had been revoked. In such circumstances, the donee does not incur any liability either to the donor or to any other person.

Subsection (2) confers protection on a third party who deals with a donee of a power which has been revoked without that third party's knowledge of the revocation. It is, therefore, essential that notice that the power has been revoked should be given to anyone who might rely on it.

Subsection (3) refers to powers which are expressed to be irrevocable and given by way of security (see section 20, below, p. 27).

Subsection (4) is similar to section 13(4), with some differences. Section 13 deals with the protection of attorneys and third persons where a registered enduring power is invalid and not in force, while section 18 deals with the protection of donees and other persons where a power has been revoked. The protection give by section 18 to third parties must be qualified in respect of enduring powers by the fact that their revocation becomes valid when confirmed by the court. Thus, a person relying on an enduring power should check the register to ensure that the registration of the enduring power has not been revoked. The provisions of section 13(5) are relevant here.

The presumption in section 18(4) is that the purchaser "did not at the material time know of the revocation of the power" whereas the presumption in section 13(4) is "that the transaction was valid". Subparagraph (b) in section 18(4) provides that the statutory declaration must state that the purchaser "did not at the material time know of the revocation of the power" whereas subparagraph (b) of section 13(4) provides that the declaration must state that that person "had no reason at the time of transaction to doubt that the attorney had authority to dispose of the property which was the subject of the transaction".

Subsection (5) gives further protection to a person dealing with the donee of a power without knowledge of the occurrence of any event which has the effect of revoking the power.

Subsection (6) contains the definition of "purchaser" which is similar to the definition of "purchaser" in the Conveyancing Acts, but "includes also an intending purchaser". The subsection (6) definition of purchaser includes the ingredient of "good faith" which does not appear in the definition of purchaser in section 1 of the Conveyancing Act 1882. Presumably, the presumption contained in section 18(4) overrides any constructive notice which a purchaser might be deemed to have under section 3 of the Conveyancing Act 1882 (see Wylie, *op. cit.*, above, paras 3.072 *et seq.*).

Subsection (7) applies section 18 to powers of attorney whenever created, but only to acts and transactions after the commencement of that section.

Protection of transferee under stock exchange transaction

19.—(1) Without prejudice to section 18, where—
   (a) the donee of a power of attorney executes, as transferor, an instrument transferring registered securities, and
   (b) the instrument is executed for the purposes of a stock exchange transaction,

it shall be presumed in favour of the transferee unless the contrary is shown that the power had not been revoked at the date of the instrument if a statutory declaration to that effect is made by the donee of the power on or within three months after that date.

(2) In this section "registered securities" and "stock exchange transaction" have the same meanings as in the Stock Transfer Act, 1963.

GENERAL NOTE

Section 19 applies to enduring powers and to ordinary powers of attorney. It confers special protection on the transferee of registered securities which are transferred by the donee of a power of attorney for the purposes of a stock exchange transaction. The section creates a presumption in favour of such a transferee (unless the contrary is shown) that the power had not been revoked at the date of the instrument, if a statutory declaration to that effect is made by the donee of the power on or within three months after that date. "Registered securities" and "stock exchange transactions" have the same meanings as in the Stock Transfer Act 1963. This section mirrors section 6(1) of the U.K. Powers of Attorney Act 1971, except in one important respect. In the U.K. section the presumption is "conclusive" while in the Irish section the presumption is "unless the contrary is shown".

Power given as security

20.—(1) Where a power of attorney is expressed to be irrevocable and is given to secure—
   (a) a proprietary interest of the donee of the power, or
   (b) the performance of an obligation owed to the donee,
then, so long as the donee has that interest or the obligation remains undischarged, the power shall not be revoked—
   (i) by the donor without the consent of the donee, or
   (ii) by the death, incapacity or bankruptcy of the donor or, if the donor is a body corporate, by its winding-up or dissolution.

(2) A power of attorney given to secure a proprietary interest may be given, and shall be deemed to have been capable always of being given, to the person entitled to the interest and persons deriving title under that person to that interest, and those persons shall be duly constituted donees of the power for all purposes of the power but without prejudice to any right to appoint substitutes given by the power.

(3) This section applies to powers of attorney whenever created.

Powers of Attorney Act 1996

GENERAL NOTE

Section 20 confirms the law relating to powers of attorney given for security, where the power of attorney is expressed to be irrevocable and is given to secure a proprietary interest of the donee of the power, or the performance of an obligation owed to the donee. So long as the donee has that interest, or the obligation remains undischarged, power shall not be revoked:
1. By the donor, without the consent of the donee; or
2. By the death, incapacity or bankruptcy of the donor, or if the donor is a body corporate, by its winding up or dissolution.

Subsection (2) provides a power of attorney given to secure a proprietary interest will run with the ownership of that interest and the person entitled to the interest; and persons still having title under that person to that interest, which shall be duly constituted donees of the power for all purposes of the power, but without prejudice to any right to appoint substitutes given by the power. This section applies to powers of attorney whenever created. It is unlikely that this section can apply to enduring powers because they cannot be "expressed to be irrevocable". The statutory instrument providing for the form of enduring powers does not envisage such a provision.

Section 5 of the Family Law (Miscellaneous Provisions) Act 1997 amended section 20 of the 1996 Act, by the substitution of the following subsection for subsection (3).

> "(3) This section does not apply to a power of attorney that was given otherwise than to secure an interest, or the performance of an obligation, referred to in subsection (1) and was created by an instrument executed before the 1st day of August 1996, but, subject to the foregoing, applies to powers of attorney whenever created".

This amendment is obscure and the Explanatory Memorandum does not appear to throw any light on it. It ensures, certainly, that irrevocable powers of attorney given prior to the enactment of the Powers of Attorney Act 1996, otherwise than to secure an interest, or performance of an obligation, are not affected by section 20. Reasons for the amendment of subsection (3) were given by the Minister of State at the Department of Enterprise and Employment, (see 478 *Dáil Debates* Cols. 325–326 (Second Stage). The Minister stated:

> "Section 20 of the 1996 Act made it clear the only powers which ought to be irrevocable should be those given by way of security, for example, to protect a mortgagee in the event of default in repayments by the Donor of the Power. This Section applies to Powers of Attorney whenever created. When the 1996 Act was introduced, it was widely understood there were no cases where Powers of Attorney had been granted otherwise than by way of security. However the attention of the Minister for Equality and Law Reform has recently been drawn to a case where a person had given a Power of Attorney which was expressed to be irrevocable and was in consideration of an annual payment to the donees. The intention of the donor was that the donees should be in a position to act in the event of the donor's incapacity. Legal advice was obtained by the parties to the effect that the power was valid under Section 8 of the 1882 Act (the Conveyancing Act, 1882). Although there may be other similar cases none have so far been reported. The Minister for Equality and Law Reform is of the view that any power of attorney given before the date on which the 1996 Act came into operation under the 1882 Act, otherwise than by way of security, should not be so affected by section 20 of the 1996 Act. Accordingly he has provided in section 5 that section 20 shall not invalidate powers of attorney given otherwise than by way of security under sections 8 and 9 of the 1882 Act".

Proof of instrument creating power

21.—(1) A power of attorney may be proved by production of the original instrument or of a copy which—

(a) is certified by the donor of the power or by a solicitor or member firm (within the meaning of the Stock Exchange Act, 1995), or in such other manner as the court approves, to be a true copy of the original, or

(b) where the instrument has been deposited in the Central Office of the High Court pursuant to section 22 is attested in accordance with that section.

(2) It is immaterial for the purposes of subsection (1) how many removes there are between the copy and the original or by what means (which may include facsimile transmission) the copy produced or any intermediate copy was made.

(3) This section is without prejudice to any other method of proof authorised by law.

GENERAL NOTE

Section 21 introduces a new method of proving powers of attorney. Although this section is not excluded from applying to enduring powers, it would seem prudent to rely on section 11(5) in relation to the proof of the contents of an enduring power and the fact that it has been registered. Heretofore one had to rely on section 48(4) of the Conveyancing Act 1881 to prove the contents of a power of attorney. Section 48 is repealed by the Powers of Attorney Act 1996. Section 48(4) of the 1881 Act provided that:

> "an office copy of an instrument so deposited shall without further proof be sufficient evidence of the contents of the instrument and of the deposit thereof in the Central Office".

Thus, in order to prove a power of attorney prior to the 1996 Act, one had to produce either the original or a Central Office certified copy thereof. In Land Registry dealings, the original power of attorney, or the Central Office certified copy, had to be lodged in the Land Registry and a solicitors certified copy would not suffice.

Section 21 provides that a power of attorney may be proved by the production of the original instrument or of a copy certified by the donor, or by a solicitor, or by a member firm (within the meaning of the Stock Exchange Act 1995), or in such other manner as the court approves. Alternatively, where the instrument has been deposited in the Central Office in the High Court, pursuant to section 22 of the 1996 Act, it may be proved by a copy attested in accordance with that section. Convenience would therefore appear to dictate that a power of attorney should not be deposited in the Central Office, because in such circumstances a copy thereof certified in accordance with section 21(1)(a) will not suffice.

Section 21(2) further facilitates proof of a power of attorney, by providing that it is immaterial how many removes there are between the copy and the original, or by what means the copy was produced, or any intermediate copy thereof was made. Subsection (2) can presumably only apply to powers of attorney which have not been deposited in the Central Office.

It is not provided that this section applies to powers of attorney whenever executed. In the light of the provision of section 22(6) it must be assumed that section 21 only applies to powers of attorney created after the 1996 Act came into operation.

Deposit of original instruments in Central Office

22.—(1) An instrument creating a power of attorney, its execution being verified by affidavit, statutory declaration or other sufficient evidence, may, with the affidavit or declaration, if any, be deposited in the Central Office of the High Court.

(2) A separate file of instruments so deposited shall be kept and any person

may, free of charge during normal office hours, search that file and inspect any instrument so deposited, and an attested copy thereof shall be delivered to that person on request.

(3) A copy of an instrument so deposited may be presented at the Central Office, and may be stamped or marked as an attested copy, and when so stamped or marked shall become and be an attested copy.

(4) An attested copy of an instrument so deposited shall without further proof be sufficient evidence of the contents of the instrument and of the deposit thereof in the Central Office.

(5) Subsections (2) to (4) apply to instruments deposited in the Central Office before the commencement of this section.

(6) This section applies to instruments creating powers of attorney whenever executed.

GENERAL NOTE

Section 22 mirrors section 48 of the Conveyancing Act 1881 (see above). Subsection (5) was added after the Committee Stage of the Bill had been concluded by the Select Committee on Legislation and Security. It is difficult to understand why subsection (5) is necessary having regard to subsection (6).

It is understood that representations were made by the Law Society Conveyancing Committee to the Minister to drop section 22 entirely, or make it mandatory. Many feel that section 22 creates confusion, with some practitioners insisting that all powers of attorney be deposited in the Central Office, while others point to the fact that section 22 is not mandatory. In practice, some solicitors have insisted that powers of attorney be deposited in the Central Office, notwithstanding the fact that this does not add to the validity of the power in any way. It could be said that the only advantage to depositing a power of attorney in the Central Office is that if the power of attorney is lost an attested copy can be obtained. It is, however, clear that section 22 is not mandatory and that powers of attorney do not have to be deposited in the Central Office to be valid.

At common law the certified copy is not proof of the truth of the contents or as to the genuineness of the execution of the document creating the power (see *O'Kane v. Mullan* (1925) N.I. 1 and *Re Airey* (1897) 1 Ch. 164). Note that while section 22 refers to the proof of the contents of the power of attorney, section 21 refers merely to the proof of the power of attorney. Does an attested copy of a deposited instrument thus have an advantage over a certified copy power which has not been deposited?

Furnishing to purchaser of power relating to land

23.—A purchaser of any estate or interest in land is entitled to have any instrument creating a power of attorney which affects title thereto, or a certified copy or attested copy thereof, furnished by the vendor to the purchaser free of expense.

GENERAL NOTE

It is noteworthy that this section is not restricted to cases where the vendor is selling under power of attorney. It would seem to apply to all cases where a power of attorney affects title to land.

PART IV

MISCELLANEOUS

Laying of orders and regulations before Houses of Oireachtas

24.—Every order and regulation made under this Act shall be laid before each House of the Oireachtas as soon as may be after it is made and, if a resolution annulling the order or regulation is passed by either such House within the next subsequent twenty-one days on which the House has sat after the order or regulation is laid before it, the order or regulation shall be annulled accordingly but without prejudice to the validity of anything previously done thereunder.

GENERAL NOTE

This is the usual section relating to orders and regulations made under the Powers of Attorney Act 1996.

Repeals

25.—Each enactment specified in the Fourth Schedule is hereby repealed to the extent specified in the third column of that Schedule.

GENERAL NOTE

The Fourth Schedule lists sections 46, 47 and 48 of the Conveyancing Act 1881 and sections 8 and 9 of the Conveyancing Act 1882. This section was amended and replaced by section 5 of the Family Law (Miscellaneous Provisions) Act 1997 which provides for the substitution of the following section for section 25:

> "25. Subject to section 20(3), each enactment specified in the Fourth Schedule is hereby repealed to the extent specified in the third column of that Schedule".

Sections 9, 10, 14   FIRST SCHEDULE

NOTIFICATION PRIOR TO REGISTRATION

PART I

Duty to give Notice to Donor and Other Persons

Duty to give Notice to Donor

1. (1) Subject to subparagraph (2), before making an application for registration the attorney shall give notice of intention to do so to the donor.

(2) Paragraph 4(2) shall apply in relation to the donor as it applies in relation to a person who is entitled to receive notice under this Schedule.

GENERAL NOTE

The form and contents of the notice to the donor are contained in paragraph 5 (see below). Paragraph 4(2) permits the attorney, before applying for registration, to make an application to the court to be dispensed from the requirement to give notice (see below).

Duty to give Notice to Other Persons

2. (1) Subject to paragraph 4—
   (a) if regulations under section 5(2) have required notice of the execution of an enduring power of attorney to be brought to the attention of specified persons, the attorney shall, before making an application for registration, give notice of intention to do so to those persons;
   (b) if any of those persons is dead or mentally incapable or his or her whereabouts cannot be reasonably ascertained, the attorney shall give notice of intention to make such an application to the other person or persons, and
   (c) if all those persons are dead or mentally incapable or their whereabouts cannot be reasonably ascertained, the attorney shall, before making such an application, give notice of intention to do so to the persons (if any) who are entitled to receive notice by virtue of paragraph 3.

(2) When giving notice pursuant to subparagraph (1) the attorney shall also give notice to the Registrar of Wards of Court of intention to apply to the court for registration of the enduring power.

GENERAL NOTE

It should be noted that regulations have been made under section 5(2) (see S.I. No. 196 of 1996).

3. (1) Subject to the limitations contained in subparagraphs (2) to (4), persons of the following classes are entitled to receive notice under paragraph 2(1)(c):
   (a) the donor's husband or wife;
   (b) the donor's children;
   (c) the donor's parents;
   (d) the donor's brothers and sisters, whether of the whole or half blood;
   (e) the widow or widower of a child of the donor;
   (f) the donor's grandchildren;
   (g) the children of the donor's brothers and sisters of the whole blood;
   (h) the children of the donor's brothers and sisters of the half blood.

(2) A person is not entitled to receive notice under this paragraph if the name or address of that person is not known to and cannot be reasonably ascertained by the attorney.

(3) Except where subparagraph (4) applies, no more than three persons are entitled to receive notice by virtue of this paragraph and, in determining the persons who are so entitled, persons falling within class (a) of subparagraph (1) are to be preferred to persons falling within class (b) of that subparagraph, persons falling within class (b) are to be preferred to persons falling within class (c) of that subparagraph; and so on.

(4) Notwithstanding the limit of three specified in subparagraph (3), where—
   (a) there is more than one person falling within any of classes (a) to (h) of subparagraph (1), and
   (b) at least one of those persons would be entitled to receive notice by virtue of this paragraph,

then, subject to subparagraph (2), all the persons falling within that class are entitled to receive notice by virtue of this paragraph.

GENERAL NOTE

In the Bill as passed by the Seanad only sub-paragraphs 3(1)(a) to (d) were included. The remaining sub-paragraphs were added by the Dáil. It is interesting to note that notwithstanding the provisions of section 5(7) an estranged spouse is still entitled to receive notice in preference to, in certain circumstances, the donor's parents, or brothers and sisters.

4. (1) An attorney shall not be required to give notice under paragraph 2 to himself or herself or to any other attorney under the power who is joining in making the application, notwithstanding that he or she or, as the case may be, the other attorney is entitled to receive notice by virtue of paragraph 3.

(2) In the case of any person who is entitled to receive notice under this Schedule, the attorney, before applying for registration, may make an application to the court to be dispensed from the requirement to give that person notice; and the court may grant the application if it is satisfied—
- (a) that it would be undesirable or impracticable for the attorney to give such notice; or
- (b) that no useful purpose is likely to be served by giving it.

GENERAL NOTE

Paragraph 4(1) relieves an attorney from giving notice to himself or herself. Subparagraph (2) empowers an attorney to apply to the courts to be dispensed from the requirement to give notice either to the donor, or to any of the persons referred to in paragraphs 2 and 3. The court may grant that application if it is satisfied either that it would be undesirable or impracticable for the attorney to give such notice, or that no useful purpose is likely to be served by giving it. Presumably this would refer to a situation where the donor's spouse is estranged.

PART II

Contents of Notices

5. A notice to the donor under this Schedule—
- (a) shall be in the prescribed form or a form to the like effect;
- (b) shall state that the attorney proposes to make an application to the court for the registration of the instrument creating the enduring power in question; and
- (c) shall inform the donor that, whilst the instrument remains registered, any revocation of the power by the donor will be ineffective unless and until the revocation is confirmed by the court.

GENERAL NOTE

In the Bill as passed by the Seanad the words "to the court", in sub-paragraph 5(b) of the Act appeared as "to the Registrar of Wards of Court" in sub-paragraph (b). It is unlikely that this change will make any difference in practice.

6. A notice to any other person under this Schedule—
- (a) shall be in the prescribed form or a form to the like effect;

(b) shall contain the statement mentioned in paragraph 5(b));
(c) shall inform the person to whom it is given that that person may object to the proposed registration by notice in writing to the Registrar of Wards of Court before the expiry of the period of five weeks beginning with the day on which the notice under this Schedule was so given; and
(d) shall specify, as the grounds on which an objection to registration may be made, the grounds set out in section 10(3).

GENERAL NOTE

This paragraph refers to notices to any person other than the donor. It is noteworthy that while paragraph 6(d) provides that a notice to any person other than the donor shall specify, as the grounds on which an objection to registration may be made; the grounds set out in section 10(3); there is no corresponding subparagraph in paragraph 5. (The Act appears to be silent on any procedure for enabling the donor to object to registration).

7. In this Part, "prescribed" means prescribed by regulations which may be made by the Minister.

GENERAL NOTE

Regulations have been made by the Minister (see Appendix A, below, p. 37).

PART III

Duty to give Notice to other Attorneys

8. (1) Subject to subparagraph (2), before making an application for registration an attorney under a joint and several power shall give notice of intention to do so to any other attorney under the power who is not joining in making the application; and paragraphs 4(2) and 6 shall apply in relation to attorneys entitled to receive notice by virtue of this paragraph as they apply in relation to persons entitled to receive notice under this Schedule.

(2) An attorney is not entitled to receive notice by virtue of this paragraph if his or her address is not known to and cannot be reasonably ascertained by the applying attorney.

GENERAL NOTE

Paragraph 8 imposes a duty on the attorney under a joint and several power, before making an application for registration, to give notice of intention to do so to any other attorney under the power who is not joining in making the application. Paragraphs 4(2) and (6) shall apply in relation to attorneys entitled to receive notice. Attorneys who are appointed, or are deemed to have been appointed, to act jointly must, by virtue of such appointment, apply jointly for registration.

PART IV

Supplementary

9. For the purposes of this Schedule a notice given by post may be sent by

prepaid registered post to the usual or last known place of residence of the person to whom it is to be given and shall be regarded as given on the day on which it was posted.

GENERAL NOTE

This paragraph provides that a notice given by post may be sent by pre-paid registered post. The First Schedule does not provide a method for giving notice, nor is such a method specified by the regulations. However if notice is given by pre-paid registered post it shall be regarded as given on the day on which it was posted. No provision is made for a case where the notice is returned undelivered. It would, perhaps, have been wiser to have empowered the Minister to make regulations in relation to the service of notice.

Section 14

SECOND SCHEDULE

JOINT AND JOINT AND SEVERAL ATTORNEYS

PART I

Joint Attorneys

1. In section 5(4), the reference to the time when the attorney executes the instrument shall be read as a reference to the time when the second or last attorney executes the instrument.

GENERAL NOTE

Section 5(4) provides that a power of attorney cannot be an enduring power unless, when executing the instrument creating it, the attorney possess certain qualifications, such as, having attained the age of 18 years.

2. In sections 5(5), 8, 10(3), 12(2) and 12(4), references to the attorney shall be read as including references to any attorney under the power and, in the case of section 12(4)(d), subject to section 14(3).

GENERAL NOTE

This paragraph applies the sections mentioned therein to any attorney appointed under the power.
Section 50(b) of the Family Law (Divorce) Act 1996 added the following paragraph 2.A:

"2.A The expiry of an enduring power of attorney effected in the circumstances mentioned in Section 5(7) shall apply only so far as it relates to an attorney who is the spouse of the donor".

PART II

Joint and Several Attorneys

3. The expiry of an enduring power of attorney effected in the circumstances mentioned in section 5(7) shall apply only so far as it relates to an attorney who is the spouse of the donor.

Powers of Attorney Act 1996

GENERAL NOTE

Section 5(7) provides that an enduring power in favour of a spouse shall, unless the power provides otherwise, be invalidated, or cease to be in force, if certain events occur subsequently, such as the annulment of the marriage. Paragraph 3 covers the situation where the spouse is a joint and several attorney, and thus section 5(7) shall apply only insofar as it relates to that spouse.

Section 16 THIRD SCHEDULE

FORM OF GENERAL POWER OF ATTORNEY

This GENERAL POWER OF ATTORNEY IS MADE THIS   day of
19   by   AB   of
I appoint CD of
[or CD of   and EF of

jointly (or jointly and severally)] to be my attorney[s] in accordance with *section 16* of the *Powers of Attorney Act, 1996.*

IN WITNESS etc.

Section 25 FOURTH SCHEDULE

ENACTMENTS REPEALED

Chapter	Short Title	Extent of Repeal
44 & 45 Vict., c. 41	Conveyancing Act, 1881	Part XI (sections 46, 47 and 48).
45 & 46 Vict., c. 39	Conveyancing Act, 1882	Sections 8 and 9.

APPENDIX A

ENDURING POWERS OF ATTORNEY REGULATIONS, 1996

(S.I. No. 196 of 1996)

I, Mervyn Taylor, Minister for Equality and Law Reform, in exercise of the powers conferred on me by section 5(2) of, and the First Schedule to, the Powers of Attorney Act, 1996 (No. 12 of 1996), hereby make the following regulations:

Citation

1. These Regulations may be cited as the Enduring Powers of Attorney Regulation

Commencement

2. These Regulations shall come into operation on the 1st day of August 1996.

Form of instrument creating enduring power

3. (a) An instrument creating an enduring power shall be in the form set out in the First Schedule to these Regulations or, if the instrument relates only to personal care decisions, in the form set out in the Second Schedule thereto.
   (b) It shall include all the explanatory information in Part A of the form and the statements in Parts D and E.

Execution

4. (a) The instrument shall be executed by both the donor and the attorney (who shall execute the instrument after the donor, but not necessarily on the same date), each in the presence of a witness, but not necessarily the same witness, who shall give his or her full name and address.
   (b) The donor shall not witness the signature of an attorney nor shall an attorney witness the signature of the donor or of another attorney.

Accounts

5. An attorney who is appointed to act on the donor's behalf in relation to property and affairs of the donor shall keep adequate accounts of the management thereof and, in particular, of any expenditure to meet the needs of persons other than the donor or to make any gifts authorised by the enduring power.

Remuneration of attorney

6. The instrument may make provision in relation to the remuneration of an attorney.

Notice to specified persons of execution of enduring power

7. (a) Notice of the execution of the enduring power by the donor shall be given by or on behalf of the donor to at least two persons named by the donor in the enduring power.

Appendix A

(b) None of them shall be an attorney under the power.
(c) At least one of them shall be –
   (i) the donor's spouse, if living with the donor, or
   (ii) if clause (i) does not apply, a child of the donor, or
   (iii) if clauses (i) and (ii) do not apply, a relative (if any) of the donor.
(d) In subparagraph (c)(iii) "relative" means a parent, brother or sister (whether of the whole or half blood) or grandchild of the donor, the widow or widower of a child of the donor or a child of the donor's brother or sister (whether of the whole or half blood).

Form of notice of execution by donor of enduring power

8. A notice of the execution of an enduring power by the donor shall be in the form set out in the Third Schedule to these Regulations.

Form of notice to donor and other persons of intention to apply for registration of enduring power

9. A notice by the attorney to the donor and other persons mentioned in paragraph 2 or 3 of the First Schedule to the Powers of Attorney Act, 1996, shall be in the form set out in the Fourth Schedule to these Regulations.

FIRST SCHEDULE

Instrument creating Enduring Power of Attorney

Prescribed Form

PART A: EXPLANATORY INFORMATION

[*Note:* 1. This Part may not be omitted from the instrument.
2. If the enduring power is to relate only to personal care decisions, the for in the Second Schedule should be used]

Notice to donor and attorneys

1. Following is a simplified explanation of what the Powers of Attorney Act 1996 provides. If you need any more guidance you or your advisers will need to look at the Act itself.

2. *Do not sign this enduring power unless you understand what it means. If you are in any doubt you should obtain legal advice.*

Effect of creating enduring power: information for donor

3. An enduring power of attorney enables you to choose a person (called an "attorney") to manage your property and affairs in the event of your becoming mentally incapable of doing so. You may choose one attorney or more than one. If you choose more than one, you must decide whether they are to be able to act:

jointly (that is, they must all act together and cannot act separately), or
jointly and severally (that is, they can all act together but they can also act separately if they wish).

In Part B of this document, at the place marked [1], show what you have decided by crossing out or omitting one of the alternatives. If you do not, the attorneys are deemed to have been appointed to act jointly.

4. If you give your attorney(s) general power in relation to all your property and affairs, they will be able to deal with your money or property and may be able to sell your house.

5. If you do not want your attorney(s) to have such wide powers, you can include any restrictions you like. For example, you can include a restriction that your attorney(s) may not sell your house. Any restrictions you choose must be written or typed at the place marked [2] in Part B of this document.

6. You may authorise the attorney(s) to take certain personal care decisions on your behalf, e.g. deciding where you shall live. If you decide to do so, you should indicate, at the place marked [3] in Part B of this document, the particular personal care decisions you want to authorise. You should also name any person you would like the attorney to consult so that the attorney can have regard to that person's views as to your wishes and feelings and as to what would be in your best interests.

7. Unless you put in a restriction preventing it, your attorney(s) will be able to use any of your money or property to benefit themselves or other people by doing what you yourself might be expected to do to provide for their needs.

8. If you specifically authorise it, your attorney(s) will also be able to use your money to make gifts, but only for reasonable amounts in relation to the value of your money and property and subject to any conditions or restrictions you may impose.

9. You may also appoint an attorney or attorneys to act in the event that the original attorney is unable or unwilling to act. Provision for such an appointment is made at the place marked [4] in Part B of this document.

10. You must give notice of the execution of the enduring power as soon as practicable to at least two persons. None of them may be an attorney under the power. At least one must be the donor's spouse, if living with the donor. If the donor is unmarried, widowed or separated, notification must be given to a child of the donor (if applicable) or otherwise to any relative (i.e. parent, sibling, grandchild, widow/er of child, nephew or niece). You should give the names and addresses of those notified at the place marked [5] in Part B of this document. The prescribed form of notice is contained in the Third Schedule to the Enduring Powers of Attorney Regulations, 1996.

11. Your attorney(s) can recover the out-of-pocket expenses of acting as your attorney(s). You may provide for the attorney's remuneration as well at the place marked [6] in Part B of this document.

12. If your attorney(s) have reason in the future to believe that you have become or are becoming mentally incapable of managing your affairs, your attorney(s) must apply to have the enduring power registered in the High Court. Once registered, an enduring power of attorney cannot be revoked effectively unless the Court confirms the revocation. You may revoke the power at any time before registration.

13. Before applying to registration of this power, your attorney(s) must give written notice of intention to do so to you and to the persons you notify of the

execution of the enduring power. You and these persons (if they are not then available, certain of your relatives) will be able to object if you or they disagree with registration. The prescribed form of notice is contained in the Fourth Schedule to the Enduring Powers of Attorney Regulations, 1996.

Effect of accepting enduring power: information for attorney

14. If you have reason in the future to believe that the donor is, or is becoming, mentally incapable of managing his or her property and affairs, you must apply to have the enduring power registered in the High Court. Before doing so you must give written notice of your intention to the Registrar of Wards of Court and also to the donor and the persons whom the donor has notified of the execution of the enduring power. (If these persons are no longer available, notice must be given to certain relatives, as specified in the Powers of Attorney Act 1996) The prescribed form of the latter notice is contained in the Fourth Schedule to the Enduring Powers of Attorney Regulations, 1996.

15. The enduring power will not come into force until it has been registered. However, once you have applied for registration you may take action under the power to maintain the donor and prevent loss to the donor's estate and maintain yourself and other persons in so far as that is permitted tinder section 6(4) of the Act. You may also make any personal care decisions permitted under the power that cannot reasonably be deferred until the application for registration has beer determined.

16. Unless there is a restriction in the enduring power preventing it, you may use the donor's money or other property for your benefit or that of other people to the following extent but no further, that is to say, by doing what the donor might be expected to do to provide for your or their needs. You may not use the donor's money to make gifts unless there is specific provision to that effect in the enduring power and then only to persons related to or connected with the donor on birth or marriage anniversaries or to charities to which the donor made or might be expected to make gifts. The amounts of any such gifts are subject to any restrictions in the enduring power and, in any event, may be only for reasonable amounts in relation to the extent of the donor's assets.

17. You are obliged to keep adequate accounts of the donor's property and affairs and to produce the accounting records to the Court if required.

18. In general, as an attorney you are in a fiduciary relationship with the donor. You must use proper care in exercising on behalf of the donor the authority given by the enduring power and you must act only within its scope. In particular, you must observe any conditions or restrictions imposed by the power and also the limits imposed by the Powers of Attorney Act, 1996.

19. You may recover the out-of-pocket expenses of acting as attorney. The enduring power may provide for remuneration for so acting.

20. You may disclaim at any time up to registration of the power. Thereafter you may do so only on notice to the donor and with the consent of the High Court.

21. After the enduring power has been registered you should notify the Registrar of Wards of Court if the donor dies or recovers.

Enduring Powers of Attorney Regulations, 1996

PART B: [TO BE COMPLETED BY THE "DONOR" (THE PERSON APPOINTING THE ATTORNEY(S))]

Do not sign this form unless you understand what it means. If you are in any doubt you should obtain legal advice.

[Donor's name and address	I, _____
	of _____
Donor's date of birth	born on _____
Name(s) and address(es) of attorney(s)	appoint _____
See note 1 in Part A of this form. If you are appointing only one attorney you should cross out everything between the square brackets.	of _____
	[and _____
	of _____
*Delete the one which does not apply (see note 1 in Part A of this form).	[l]*jointly *jointly and severally]
	to act as attorney(s) for the purpose of Part II of the Powers of Attorney Act, 1996
*Delete the one which does not apply (see note 2 in Part A of this form).	*with general authority to act on my behalf
If you do not want the attorney(s) to have general power, you must give details here of what authority you are giving the attorney(s).	*with authority to do the following on my behalf:
	in relation to
*Delete the one which does not apply	*all my property and affairs
If you choose the second alternative you must give details here of the property and affairs	*the following property and affairs
in relation to which the power is to apply.	
If there are restrictions or conditions, insert them here; if not, delete these words (see note 5 in Part A of this document).	[[2] subject to the following restrictions and conditions:]
	*[[3] and with authority to take on my behalf decisions on the following matters:
	*where I should live *with whom I should live *whom I should see and not see *what training or rehabilitation I shouldget *my diet and dress *inspection of my personal papers *housing, social services and other benefits for me.]
*Delete if not applicable.	*[_____ [and _____]should be consulted for his/her/their views as to wishes and feelings and as to what would be in my best interests.]

Appendix A

[[4] I appoint _____

of _____

[and _____

of _____

*Delete this provision if, or to the extent, not required.

*jointly
*jointly and severally]

to act as attorney(s) if an attorney appointed by this instrument dies or is unable or declines to act or is disqualified from acting as attorney.]

[5] I am required to give notice of the execution of this power to at least two persons. I shall notify the following persons accordingly:

_____

The two or more persons to be notified may not include an attorney under the power. One must be a person selected as mentioned in note 10 of Part A of this document.

of _____
_____

of _____
_____

of _____
_____

*Delete if not applicable

*[6] My attorney(s) may be paid the following remuneration:

_____

I intend this power to be effective during any subsequent mental incapacity of mine.

I have read or have had read to me the information in paragraphs 1 to 13 of Part A of this document.

Your signature
Date

Signed by me _____
on _____

Signature of witness

In the presence of _____
Full name of witness _____
Address of witness _____
_____
_____
_____

Your attorney(s) cannot be your witness. If you are married it is not advisable for your husband or wife to be your witness.)

[*Note* – Anything in this Part in square brackets is for guidance only and may be retained, deleted or omitted as appropriate.]

Enduring Powers of Attorney Regulations, 1996

PART C: [TO BE COMPLETED BY THE ATTORNEY(S)]

[This form may be adapted to provide for sealing by a trust corporation with its common seal.]

[if there are more than two attorneys attach an additional Part C.]

Do not sign this form unless you understand what it means. If you are in any doubt you should obtain legal advice. Do not sign the form before the donor has signed Part B.

I understand my duties and obligations as attorney, including my duty to apply to the High Court for the registration of this instrument under the Powers of Attorney Act, 1996, when the donor is, or is becoming, mentally incapable, my limited power to use the donor's property to benefit persons other than the donor and my obligation to keep adequate accounts in relation to the management and disposal of the donor's property for production to the High Court if required.

I have read or have had read to me the information in paragraphs 1, 2 and 14 to 21 of Part A of this document.

[Individuals disqualified from acting as attorney are bankrupts, persons convicted of certain offences or disqualified under the Companies Acts or owning or connected with the management or operation of a nursing home in which the donor resides.

I am not a minor or otherwise disqualified from acting as attorney.

Signature of attorney _____

Date on _____

in the presence of _____

Signature of witness Full name of witness _____
Each attorney must sign the form and each
signature must be witnessed. The donor may Address of witness _____
not be the witness and one attorney may not
witness the signature of another.] _____

[To be completed only if there is a second attorney

[I understand my duties and obligations as attorney, including my duty to apply to the High Court for the registration of this instrument under the Powers of Attorney 1996, when the donor is, or is becoming, mentally incapable, my limited power to use the donor's property to benefit persons other than the donor and my obligation to keep adequate accounts in relation to the management and disposal of the donor's property for production to the High Court if required.

I have read or have had read to me the information in paragraphs 1, 2 and 14 to 21 of Part A of this document.

Appendix A

	I am not a minor or otherwise disqualified from acting as attorney.
Signature of attorney	_____
Date	_____
Signature of witness	in the presence of_____
	Full name of witness _____
Each attorney must sign the form and each signature must be witnessed. The donor may not be the witness and one attorney may not witness the signature of another.]	Address of witness_____]
	[I understand my duties and obligations if I have to act as attorney, including my duty to apply to the High Court for the registration of this instrument under the Powers of Attorney Act, 1996, when the donor is, or is becoming, mentally incapable, my limited power to use the donor's property to benefit persons other than the donor and my obligation to keep adequate accounts in relation to the management and disposal of the donor's property for production to the High Court if required.
[To be completed only if the donor is appointing a person to act as attorney if an original attorney is unable or unwilling to act	
	I have read or have had read to me the information in paragraphs 1, 2 and 14 to 21 of Part A of this document.
Signature	_____
Date	on _____
Signature of witness]	in the presence of_____
	Full name of witness _____
[To be completed only if a second person is being so appointed	[I understand my duties and obligations if I have to act as attorney, including my duty to apply to the High Court for the registration of this instrument under the Powers of Attorney Act, 1996, when the donor is, or is becoming, mentally incapable, my limited powers to use the donor's property to benefit persons other than the donor and my obligation to keep adequate accounts in relation to the management and disposal of the donor's property for production to the High Court if required.
	I have read or have had read to me the information in paragraphs 1, 2 and 14 to 21 of Part A of this document.
Signature	_____
Date	on _____
Signature of witness]	in the presence of_____
	Full name of witness _____

[*Note* – Anything in this Part in square brackets is for guidance only and may be retained, deleted or omitted as appropriate.]

Enduring Powers of Attorney Regulations, 1996

PART D: STATEMENT BY SOLICITOR

I, _____ , Solicitor, of
_____ hereby state that after
interviewing the donor [and making any necessary enquiries]* I am
satisfied that _____ (the donor) understood the effect of
creating the enduring power and I have no reason to believe that this
document is being executed by the donor as a result of fraud or undue
pressure.

*Delete if enquiries not necessary.

Signed _____

Date _____

[*Note* – This Part may not be omitted from the instrument.]

PART E: STATEMENT BY REGISTERED MEDICAL PRACTITIONER

I, _____ , a registered medical
practitioner, of _____ hereby state that
in my opinion at the time this document was executed by the donor
_____* had the mental capacity, with the assistance of
such explanations as may have been given to the donor, to
understand
the effect of creating the power.

*Name of donor

Signed _____

Date _____

[*Note* – This Part may not be omitted from the instrument.]

Appendix A

SECOND SCHEDULE

Instrument creating Enduring Power of Attorney
(personal care decisions only)

Prescribed Form

PART A: EXPLANATORY INFORMATION

[*Note* – This Part may not be omitted from the instrument.]

Notice to donor and attorneys

1. Following is a simplified explanation of what the Powers of Attorney Act. 1996 provides. If you need any more guidance you or your advisers will need to look at the Act itself.

2. Do not sign this enduring power unless you understand what it means. If you are in any doubt you should obtain legal advice.

Effect of creating enduring power: information for donor

3. This form of enduring power of attorney enables you to choose a person (called an "attorney") to make certain personal care decisions on your behalf in the event of your becoming mentally incapable. You may choose one attorney or more than one. If you choose more than one, you must decide whether they are to be able to act:

> **jointly** (that is, they must all act together and cannot act separately), or
> **jointly and severally** (that is, they can all act together but they can also act separately if they wish).

In Part B of this document, at the place marked [11, show what you have decided by crossing out or omitting one of the alternatives. If you do not, the attorneys are deemed to have been appointed jointly.

4. The personal care decisions that you may authorise your attorney(s) to make on your behalf are as follows:

> where you should live
> with whom you should live
> whom you should see and not see
> what training or rehabilitation you should get
> your diet and dress
> inspection of your personal papers
> housing, social welfare and other benefits for you.

5. You should indicate, at the place marked [2] in Part B of this document, the particular personal care decisions you want to authorise. You should also name any person you would like the attorney to consult so that the attorney can have regard to that person's views as to your wishes and feelings and as to what would be in your best interests.

6. You may also appoint an attorney or attorneys to act in the event that the original attorney is unable or unwilling to act. Provision for such an appointment

is made at the place marked [3] in Part B of this document.

7. You must give notice of the execution of the enduring power as soon as practicable to at least two persons. None of them may be an attorney under the power. At least one must be the donor's spouse, if living with the donor. If the donor is unmarried, widowed or separated, notification must be given to a child of the donor (if applicable) or otherwise to any relative (i.e. parent, sibling, grand-child, widow/er of child, nephew or niece You should give the names and addresses of those notified at the place marked [4] in Part B of this document. The prescribed form of notice is contained in the Third Schedule to the Enduring Powers of Attorney Regulations, 1996.

8. Your attorney(s) can recover the out-of-pocket expenses of acting as your attorney(s). You may provide for the attorney's remuneration, and who is to pay it, at the place marked [5] in Part B of this document.

9. If your attorney(s) have reason in the future to believe that you have become or are becoming mentally incapable of managing your affairs, your attorney(s) must apply to have the enduring power registered in the High Court. Once registered, an enduring power of attorney cannot be revoked effectively unless the Court confirms the revocation. You may revoke the power at any time before registration.

10. Before applying for registration of this power, your attorney(s) must give written notice of intention to do so to you and to the persons you notify of the execution of the enduring power. You and these persons (if they are not then available. certain of your relatives) will be able to object if you or they disagree with registration. The prescribed form of notice is contained in the Fourth Schedule to the Enduring Powers of Attorney Regulations, 1996.

Effect of accepting enduring power: information for attorney

11. I you have reason in the future to believe that the donor is, or is becoming, mentally incapable of managing his or her property and affairs, you must apply to have the enduring power registered in the High Court. Before doing so you must give written notice of your intention to the Registrar of Wards of Court and also to the donor and the persons whom the donor has notified of the execution of the enduring power. (if these persons are no longer available, notice must be given to certain relatives, as specified in the Powers of Attorney Act 1996.) The prescribed form of the latter notice is contained in the Fourth Schedule to the Enduring Powers of Attorney Regulations, 1996.

12. The enduring power will not come into force until it has been registered. However, once you have applied for registration you may make any personal care decisions permitted under the power that cannot reasonably be deferred until the application for registration has been determined.

13. Any personal decision you make on behalf of the donor must be made in the donor's best interests. Section 6(7)(b) of the 1996 Act provides the following guidance in this respect:

> "In deciding what is in a donor's best interests regard shall be had to the following:
> (i) so far as ascertainable, the past and present wishes and feelings of the donor and the factors which the donor would consider if he or she were able to do so;

(ii) the need to permit and encourage the donor to participate, or to improve the donor's ability to participate, as fully as possible in any decision affecting the donor;
(iii) so far as it is practicable and appropriate to consult any of the persons mentioned below, their views as to the donor's wishes and feelings and as to what would be in the donor's best interests:
  (I) any person named by the donor as someone to be consulted on those matters;
  (II) anyone (whether the donor's spouse, a relative, friend or other person) engaged in caring for the donor or interested in the donor's welfare;
(iv) whether the purpose for which any decision is required can be as effectively achieved in a manner Ass restrictive of the donor's freedom of action."

Section 6(7) further provides that in the case of any personal care decision made by an attorney it shall be a sufficient compliance with this provision if the attorney reasonably believes that what he or she decides is in the best interests of the donor.

14. You may recover the out-of-pocket expenses of acting as attorney. The enduring power may provide for remuneration for so acting.

15. You may disclaim at any time up to registration of the power. Thereafter you may do so only on notice to the donor and with the consent of the High Court.

16. After the enduring power has been registered you should notify the Registrar of Wards of Court if the donor dies or recovers.

PART B: [TO BE COMPLETED BY THE "DONOR" (THE PERSON APPOINTING THE ATTORNEY(S))]

Do not sign this form unless you understand what it means. If you are in any doubt you should obtain legal advice.

[Donor's name and address	I, _____
	of _____
Donor's date of birth	born on _____
Name(s) and address(es) of attorney(s)	appoint _____
	of _____
	[and _____
See note 3 in Part A of this document If you are appointing only one attorney you should delete everything between the square brackets.	of _____
*Delete the one which does not apply (see note 3 in Part A of this document).	[l]*jointly 　*jointly and severally]
	to act as attorney[s] for the purposes of Part II of the Powers of Attorney Act, 1996
	[2] with authority to take on my behalf decisions on the following matters:

Enduring Powers of Attorney Regulations, 1996

Delete if not applicable.

*where I should live
*with whom I should live
*whom I should see and not see
*what training or rehabilitation I should get
*my diet and dress
*inspection of my personal papers
*housing, social services and other benefits for me.]
[_____ [and_____] should be consulted for his/her/their views as to my wishes and feelings and as to what would be in my best interests.]

[[3] I appoint _____
of _____
[and _____
of _____

Delete this provision if, or to the extent, not required.

*jointly
*jointly and severally)

to act as attorney(s) if an attorney appointed by this instrument disclaims or dies or is unable to act or is disqualified from acting as attorney.]

[4] I am required to give notice of the execution of this power to at least two persons. I shall notify the following persons accordingly:

_____
of _____

The two or more persons to be notified may not include an attorney under the power. One must be a person selected as mentioned in note 7 of Part A of this document.

_____
of _____

_____
of _____

*Delete if not applicable.

*[5] My attorney(s) may be paid the following remuneration:

_____

Name of payer

by_____.]

I intend that this power shall continue even if I become mentally incapable.

I have read or have had read to me the information in paragraphs 1 to 10 of Part A of this document.

Your signature

Signed by me _____

Date

on _____

Appendix A

Someone must witness your signature

Your attorney(s) cannot be your witness. If you are married it is not advisable for your husband or wife to be your witness.]

In the presence of _____
Full name of witness _____
Address of witness _____
_____
_____
_____

[*Note* – Anything in this Part in square brackets is for guidance only and may be retained, deleted or omitted as appropriate.]

PART C: [TO BE COMPLETED BY THE ATTORNEY(S)]

[This form may be adapted to provide for scaling by a trust corporation with its common seal.]

[If there are more than two attorneys attac an additional Part C.]

Do not sign this farm unless you understand what it means. If you are in any doubt you should obtain legal advice. Do not sign the form before the donor has signed Part B.

[Individuals disqualified from acting as attorney are bankrupts, persons convicted of certain offences or disqualified under the Companies Acts or owning or connected with the management or operation of a nursing home in which the donor resides.

Signature of attorney

Date

Signature of witness

Each attorney must sign the form and each signature must be witnessed. The donor may not be the witness and one attorney may not witness the signature of another.]

I understand my duties and obligations as attorney, including my duty to apply to the High Court for the registration of this instrument under the Powers of Attorney Act, 1996, when the donor is, or is becoming, mentally incapable, and that any personal care decisions made by me on behalf of the donor must be made in the donor's best interests.

I have read or have had read to me the information in paragraphs 1, 2 and 11 to 16 of Part A of this document.

I am not a minor or otherwise disqualified from acting as attorney.

_____

_____

in the presence of _____
Full name of witness _____
Address of witness _____
_____
_____

I understand my duties and obligations as attorney, including my duty to apply to the High Court for the registration of this

Enduring Powers of Attorney Regulations, 1996

[To be completed only if there is a second attorney

See note above regarding disqualified persons.

Signature of attorney

Date

Signature of witness

Each attorney must sign the form and each signature must be witnessed. The donor may not be the witness and one attorney may not witness the signature of another.]

[To be completed only if the donor is appointing a person to act as attorney if an original attorney is unable of unwilling to act

See note above regarding isqualified persons.

Signature

Date

Signature of witness]

[To be completed only if a second person is being so appointed.

instrument under the Powers of Attorney Act, 1996, when the donor is, or is becoming, mentally incapable, and that any personal care decisions made by me on behalf of the donor must be made in the donor's best interests.

I have read or have had read to me the information in paragraphs 1, 2 and 11 to 16 of Part A of this document.

I am not a minor or otherwise disqualified from acting as attorney.

_____

_____

in the presence of _____

Full name of witness _____

Address of witness _____

[I understand my duties and obligations if I have to act as attorney, including my duty to apply to the High Court for the registration of this instrument under the Attorrney Act, 1996, when the donor is, or is becoming, mentally incapable, and that any personal care decisions made by me on the donor's behalf must be made in the donor's best interests.

I have read or have had read to me the information in paragraphs 1, 2 and 11 to 16 of Part A of this document.

I am not a minor or otherwise disqualified from acting as attorney.

_____

on _____

in the presence of _____

Full name of witness _____

Address of witness _____

[I understand my duties and obligations if I have to act as attorney, including my duty to apply to he High Court for the registration of this instrument under the Powers of Attorney Act, 1996, when the donor is, or is becoming, mentally incapable, and that any personal care decisions made by me on he donor's behalf must be made in the donor's best interests.

Appendix A

	I have read or have had read to me the information in paragraphs 1, 2 and 11 to 16 of Part A of this document.
See note above regarding disqualified persons.	I am not a minor or otherwise disqualified from acting as attorney.
Signature	
Date	on _____
Signature of witness]	in the presence of _____
	Full name of witness _____
	Address of witness _____

[*Note* – Anything in this Part in square brackets is for guidance only and may be retained, deleted or omitted as appropriate.]

PART D: STATEMENT BY SOLICITOR

I, _____, Solicitor, of _____ hereby state that after

*Delete if enquiries not necessary.

interviewing the donor [and making any necessary enquiries]* I am satisfied that _____ (the donor) understood the effect of creating the enduring power and I have no reason to believe that this document is being executed by the donor as a result of fraud or undue pressure.

Signed _____

Date _____

[*Note* – This Part may not be omitted from the instrument.]

PART E: STATEMENT BY REGISTERED MEDICAL PRACTITIONER

I, _____, a registered medical practitioner, of _____ hereby state that in my opinion at the time this document was executed by the donor

*Name of donor

_____* had the mental capacity, with the assistance

such explanations as may have been given to the donor, to understand
the effect of creating the power.

Signed _____

Date _____

[*Note* – This Part may not be omitted from the instrument.]

Enduring Powers of Attorney Regulations, 1996

THIRD SCHEDULE

ENDURING POWERS OF ATTORNEY REGULATIONS, 1996

Notice of execution by donor of enduring power

To _____
of _____
_____

[Name of donor TAKE NOTICE that I, _____
Address of donor of _____
_____

executed on _____ 19 ____ an instrument creating an enduring power of attorney and appointing

Name of attorney	_____
Address of attorney	of _____
	_____
Delete words in brackets if you have appointed only one attorney	[and _____ of _____ to act as my attorney(s) if I should become mentally incapacitated.
Signature of donor]	Signed _____ Date _____

Information for donor

1. You must give notice of the execution of the enduring power to at least two people.

2. None of the persons to be notified may be an attorney under the enduring power.

3. At last one must be your spouse, W living with you. If you are unmarried, widowed or separated, notification must be given to your child (if applicable) or otherwise to any relative (i.e. parent, sibling, grandchild, widow/er of child, nephew or niece).

4. *It is advisable that this notice be sent by prepaid registered post and that the certificate of posting be kept In a safe place.*

Information for recipient of notice

1. The enduring power will not come into force until the donor is, or is becoming, mentally incapable of managing his or her property and affairs and until it has been registered in the High Court.

2. Notice of intention to apply for registration of the enduring power will be given to you before the attorney applies for registration.

[*Note* – The words in square brackets in the margin of the form may be omitted.]

Appendix A

FOURTH SCHEDULE

ENDURING POWERS OF ATTORNEY REGULATIONS, 1996

Notice of intention to apply for registration

To _____

of _____

Name of attorney(s)   TAKE NOTICE that I/we _____

_____

Address(es) of   of _____
attorney(s)
_____

_____

_____

Name of donor   the attorney(s) of _____

Address of   (hereinafter called "the donor") of _____
donor
_____

_____

propose to apply to the High Court for the registration of the instrument creating the enduring power of attorney appointing me/us attorney(s) and executed by the donor on the ____ 19 __.

1. You have 5 weeks from the date on which this notice is given to object in writing to the proposed registration of the enduring power. Objections should be sent to the Registrar of Wards of Court, Four Courts, Dublin 7 and should contain the following details:
    (a) your name and address,
    (b) if you are not the donor, the name and address of the donor,
    (c) any relationship to the donor,
    (d) the name and address of the attorney, and
    (e) the grounds for objecting to the registration of the enduring power.

2. You may object to the registration of the enduring power on any one or more of the following grounds:
    (a) that the enduring power purported to have been created was not valid;
    (b) that the enduring power is no longer a valid and subsisting power;
    (c) that the donor is not, or is not becoming, mentally incapable;
    (d) that, having regard to all the circumstances, the attorney is unsuitable to be the donor's attorney;
    (e) that fraud or undue pressure was used to induce the donor to create the enduring power.

Enduring Powers of Attorney Regulations, 1996

Delete this paragraph if the notice is addressed to a person other than the donor.	3. You are informed that while the enduring power remains registered you will not be able to revoke it unless and until the Court confirms the revocation.
The notice should be signed by all the attorneys who are applying to register theenduring power.	Signed _____ Signed _____ Date _____

Notice to attorney(s):

1. This notice must be given to the donor and also to the other persons who were notified of the execution of the enduring power and are named in it.
2. If any of those persons are dead or mentally incapable or their whereabouts cannot be reasonably ascertained. the notice must be given to the other person or persons who were so notified.
3. If all of those persons are dead or mentally incapable or their whereabouts cannot be reasonably ascertained, the notice must be given to the relatives (if any) who are entitled to receive notice by virtue of paragraph 3 of the First Schedule of the Powers of Attorney Act 1996.
4. You must also give notice to the Registrar of Wards of Court of your intention to apply to the Court for registration of the power at the same time as you are giving notice to the donor and those other persons. A copy of each of the notices should be enclosed for the Registrar's information.

[*Note* – The words in square brackets in the margin of the form may be omitted.]

APPENDIX B

ENDURING POWERS OF ATTORNEY (PERSONAL CARE DECISIONS) REGULATIONS, 1996

(S.I. No. 287 of 1996)

I, Mervyn Taylor, Minister for Equality and Law Reform, in exercise of the powers conferred on me by section 5(2) of the Powers of Attorney Act, 1996 (No. 12 of 1996), hereby make the following regulations:

1. These Regulations may be cited as the Enduring Powers of Attorney (Personal Care Decisions) Regulations, 1996.

2. These Regulations shall come into operation on the 7th day of October, 1996.

3. (1) The Enduring Powers of Attorney Regulations, 1996 (S.I. No. 196 of 1996), are hereby amended by the deletion from Part B of the Second Schedule of the sentence I intend that this power shall continue even if I become mentally incapable" and the substitution of the following: I intend this power to be effective during any subsequent mental incapacity of mine.".

(2) The said Part B, as so amended, is set out for convenience in the Annex to these Regulations.

(3) The said amendment is made without prejudice to the validity of the original form contained in instruments made before the commencement of these Regulations.

ANNEX

SECOND SCHEDULE, ENDURING POWERS OF ATTORNEY REGULATIONS, 1991 NEW PART B

PART B: [TO BE COMPLETED BY THE "DONOR" (THE PERSON APPOINTING THE ATTORNEY(S))]

Do not sign this form unless you understand what it means. If you are in any doubt you should obtain legal advice.

[Donor's name and address	I, _____
	of _____
Donor's date of birth	born on _____
Name(s) and address(es) of attorney(s)	appoint _____
See note 3 in Part A of this document If your are appointing only one attorney you should delete everything between the square brackets.	[and _____ _____
*Delete the one which does not apply (see note 3 in Part A of this document).	[l]*jointly *jointly and severally]

Appendix B

to act as attorney[s] for the purposes of Part II of the Powers of Attorney Act, 1996

[2] with authority to take on my behalf decisions on the following matters:

Delete if not applicable.

*where I should live
*with whom I should live
*whom I should see and not see
*what training or rehabilitation I should get
*my diet and dress
*inspection of my personal papers
*housing, social services and other benefits for me.]

[_____ [and_____] should be consulted for his/her/their views as to my wishes and feelings and as to what would be in my best interests.]

[[3] I appoint _____
of _____
[and _____

Delete this provision if, or to the extent, not required.

of _____

*jointly
*jointly and severally)

to act as attorney(s) if an attorney appointed by this instrument disclaims or dies or is unable to act or is disqualified from acting as attorney.]

[4] I am required to give notice of the execution of this power to at least two persons. I shall notify the following persons accordingly:

_____
of _____

The two or more persons to be notified may not include an attorney under the power. One must be a person selected as mentioned in note 7 of Part A of this document.

_____
of _____
_____

_____
of _____
_____

*Delete if not applicable.

*[5] My attorney(s) may be paid the following remuneration:

_____

Name of payer

by_____.]

I intend that this power shall continue even if I become mentally incapable.

Enduring Powers of Attorney (Personal Care Decisions) Regulations, 1996

	I have read or have had read to me the information in paragraphs 1 to 10 of Part A of this document.
Your signature	Signed by me _____
Date	on _____
	In the presence of _____
Someone must witness your signature	Full name of witness _____
	Address of witness _____
Your attorney(s) cannot be your witness. If you are married it is not advisable for your husband or wife to be your witness.]	_____ _____ _____

[*Note* – Anything in this Part in square brackets is for guidance only and may be retained, deleted or omitted as appropriate.]

APPENDIX C

PRACTICE DIRECTION

Powers of Attorney Act 1996
Enduring Powers of Attorney Regulations 1996
(S.I. No. 196 of 1996)

The above entitled Act contains provisions for applications to be made to the High Court in relation to "enduring powers of attorney" as therein defined. Pending the making of Rules of Court by the Superior Court Rules Committee the procedure to be adopted in making such applications should be as follows:

(1) Applications under sections 8, 9(1), 9(3) of the Act and paragraph 4(2) of the First Schedule to the Act should be made by Special Summons to be issued in the Central Office. The summons should be entitled;

"In the matter of the Powers of Attorney Act, 1996"

In the matter of an Instrument creating an Enduring Power of Attorney executed by A.B. of   on the   day of   19   .

On the application of
            C.D. of

It should be addressed to the "Registrar of Wards of Court". Reference to the requirement to attend before the Master contained in Form 3 of Appendix A to the 1986 Rules should be deleted and in lieu thereof the following inserted;

"No service. This Summons is issued for the purpose of obtaining an order pursuant to the provisions of the Powers of Attorney Act, 1996."

(2) The Endorsement on the summons should set out the section of the Act under which the application is brought and the relief claimed. It should be grounded on an affidavit which should contain the information set out in Schedule 1 hereto, and which should exhibit the documents set out in, Schedule 2 hereto.

(3) As soon as practicable after the issue of the Summons two copies of the Summons and of the affidavit grounding it and copies of the exhibits (certified by the applicant's solicitor as being true copies) should be delivered by hand to the office of the Registrar of Wards of Court.

(4) When an application for registration is made under section 9(1) of the Act and section 10(2) does not apply the Registrar shall proceed to register the Enduring Power of Attorney in accordance with the provisions of the Act'. When section 10 (2) applies and in the case of applications under sections 8 and section 9(3) of the Act the Registrar shall obtain the directions of the President of the High Court or a judge nominated by him as to what enquiries are to be made [when the application is made under section 9(1)], what persons should be given notice of the hearing, the date of the hearing and any other matter required to enable the court to exercise its jurisdiction under the Act. In the case of applications under paragraph 4(2) of the First Schedule to the Act the Registrar shall obtain the directions of the President or a judge nominated by him as to the date of the hearing and as to the persons (if any) who should be given notice of the hearing.

Appendix C

(5) Applications under section 12(1) and 12(3) shall be by notice of motion to be issued in the Central Office directed to the Registrar. The Registrar shall obtain the Directions of the President or of a judge nominated by him as to the persons to be served with the motion (if any), the date of the hearing, and any other matter required to enable the court to exercise its jurisdiction under the Act.

Dated:

Signed:

President of the High Court.

SCHEDULE 1

INFORMATION TO BE SET OUT IN THE AFFIDAVIT GROUNDING AN APPLICATION FOR RELIEF UNDER THE POWERS OF ATTORNEY ACT 1996

(i) The present address of the Donor and of the persons to whom notice under the Act has been given.

(ii) The date on which the EPA was executed.

(iii) The date on which Notice of Execution by the Donor was given and the persons to whom such Notice was given.

(iv) Date of Completion of Statement by Attorney (Part C of Regulations).

(v) Date of Completion of Statement by Solicitor (Part D of Regulations).

(vi) Date of Completion of Statement by Doctor (Part E of Regulations).

(vii) Date on which Notice of Intention to apply for Registration was given to the Donor.

(viii) Dates on which Notice of Intention to apply for Registration was given to the Notice persons referred to in (i) and (iii) above.

(ix) That the EPA is in the same state plight and condition as when it came into the possession of the Deponent – the manner in which it came into the possession of the Deponent to be stated.

(x) That a registered Medical Practitioner has certified that the Donor is, or is becoming, incapable by reason of a mental condition of managing his or her own property and affairs.

(xi) That there is no other person to whom notice is required to be given under paragraph 2 of the First Schedule to the Act.

(xii) Whether there is any reason to believe that appropriate enquiries might bring to light evidence on which the Court could be satisfied that one of the grounds of objection set out in section 10(3) of the Act is established.

Practice Direction

SCHEDULE 2

The following documentation (or so much thereof as shall be in existence at the time of the making of the Application and as is in the possession or procurement of the Deponent) should be exhibited in the grounding Affidavit.

(i) The EPA.

(ii) Copy notice of Execution by the Donor of the EPA given to the first notice party.

(iii) Copy notice of Execution by the Donor of the EPA given to the second notice party.

(iv) Copy notice of Execution by the Donor of the EPA given to any other notice party.

(v) Copy notice of Intention to apply for registration given to the Donor.

(vi) Copy notice of Intention to apply for registration given to the first notice party.

(vii) Copy notice of Intention to apply for registration given to the second notice party.

(viii) Copy notice of Intention to apply for registration given to any other notice party.

(ix) Affidavits of Service of the Notices referred to at paragraphs (v), (vi), (vii) and (viii).

(x) Certificate of a registered Medical Practitioner to the effect that the Donor is (or is becoming) incapable by reason of a mental condition of managing his/her property and affairs.

APPENDIX D

RULES OF THE SUPERIOR COURTS (NO. 1)
(POWERS OF ATTORNEY ACT, 1996) 2000 (S.I. No. 66 of 2000)

1. The following Order shall be inserted as Order 129 of the Rules of the Superior Courts immediately after Order 128 thereof.

2. This rule shall come into operation on the 8th day of March 2000.

3. This rule shall be construed with the Rules of the Superior Courts, 1986 to 2000 and may be cited as the Rules of the Superior Courts (No. l) (Powers of Attorney Act, 1996) 2000.

ORDER 129

POWERS OF ATTORNEY ACT, 1996

1. In this Order—

"the Act" means the Powers of Attorney Act, 1996

"the Court" means the President of the High Court or such other Judge of the High Court as may be assigned by him from time to time to hear applications under the Act and shall, where appropriate, include the Registrar.

"the Registrar" means the Registrar of Wards of Court.

"the Regulations" means the Enduring Powers of Attorney Regulations, 1996 (S.I. No. 196 of 1996) as amended by the Enduring Powers of Attorney (Personal Care Decisions) Regulations, 1996 (S.I. No. 287 of 1996).

Words and expressions shall, unless the contrary intention appears, have the same meaning as in the Act.

Pre-Registration Applications

2(1) The following applications may be made ex parse to the Court by means of an *ex parte* docket:

(a) an application pursuant to section 8 of the Act for the exercise of any power created under an enduring power of attorney prior to the registration of the instrument creating such power,

(b) an application pursuant to section 9(3) of the Act referring to the Court for its determination any question as to the validity of the power;

(c) an application pursuant to paragraph 4(2) of the First Schedule to the Act to dispense with the requirement to give notice of intention to make an application for registration under section 9 of the Act.

(2) An *ex parte* application shall be grounded upon the affidavit of the interested party or the attorney, as the case may be, and shall be lodged in the Office of the

Appendix D

Wards of Court and shall fully set forth the facts and circumstances giving rise to the application. In particular the affidavit shall contain the following matters:

    (a) the present address of the donor;

    (b) the present address or addresses of the person or persons to whom notice of execution of the power has been given;

    (c) the date on which the enduring power of attorney was executed;

    (d) the date on which notice of execution by the donor was given;

    (e) the date of completion of the statement by the attorney prescribed by Part C of the Form in the First or Second Schedule to the Regulations, as the case may be;

    (f) the date of completion of the statement by the solicitor prescribed by Part D of the Form in the First or Second Schedule to the Regulations, as the case may be;

    (g) the date of completion of the statement by the doctor prescribed by Part E of the Form required by the First or Second Schedule to the Regulations, as the case may be;

    (h) the date on which notice of intention to apply for registration was given to the donor, (if applicable);

    (i) the date or dates upon which notice of intention to apply for registration was given to the required notice parties prescribed by the Act or Regulations, (if applicable),

and the affidavit shall exhibit the power of attorney concerned and all other relevant documentation.

(3) The Court may upon such application make such order as appears appropriate in the circumstances including an order adjourning the application and directing that notice of the application be served upon any person likely to be affected thereby or may adjourn such application until it makes or causes to be made such enquiries or further enquiries, if any, as it thinks appropriate in the circumstances of the case and upon such terms and conditions as appear just.

Application for Registration

3(1) An application for the registration of an enduring power of attorney shall be made to the Registrar by lodging an application for registration in the Office of the Wards of Court and shall be grounded upon the affidavit of the attorney or attorneys seeking such registration. Such application shall, as far as practicable, be in the Form No. 1 as set out in the Appendix hereto.

(2) An affidavit grounding such an application shall fully set forth the facts and circumstances giving rise to the application. In particular the affidavit shall contain the following matters:

    (a) the present address and marital status of the donor;

    (b) the present address or addresses (if known) of the person or persons to whom notice of execution of the power has been given;

(c) the date on which the enduring power of attorney was executed (if known);

(d) the date on which notice of execution by the donor was given (if known);

(e) the date of completion of the statement by the attorney prescribed in Part C of the Form in the First or Second Schedule to the Regulations, as the case may be;

(f) the date of the completion of the statement by the solicitor prescribed by Part D of the Form in the First or Second Schedule to the Regulations, as the case may be;

(g) the date of completion of the statement by the doctor prescribed by Part E of the form required by the First or Second Schedule to the Regulations, as the case may be;

(h) the date upon which notice of intention to apply for registration was given to the donor;

(i) the date or dates upon which notice of intention to apply for registration was given to the Registrar and the required notice parties prescribed by the Act or Regulations;

(j) aver that the enduring power of attorney has not been interfered with or altered in any way since it came into the possession of the attorney and shall aver as to the date and manner in which it came into the possession of the attorney concerned;

(k) a statement that a registered medical practitioner has certified that the donor is or is becoming incapable of managing and administering his or her own property and affairs;

(l) that there is no other person to whom notice is required to be given by virtue of the provisions of the First Schedule to the Act;

and the application shall have annexed to it the power of attorney concerned, any medical certificate issued pursuant to section 9(4) of the Act, any relevant notices(or copies thereof, if available,) referred to above and any other relevant documentation.

(3) The application for registration shall be served on the donor personally and on all other parties who either have or should have received notice of an intention to apply for registration. Save for service on the donor such service may be effected by pre-paid registered post to the usual or last known place of residence of the person to whom it is to be given or by personal service or in such other substituted manner as the Court may allow as being appropriate in the circumstances on an *ex parte* application for that purpose.

(4) The Court may, or where appropriate, the Registrar may in any case require such proof of service of the notice of the applicant's intention to seek the registration or of any other notice sent or purportedly sent to any person in any case in which it appears necessary to do so and may adjourn such application until such service or notification, as the case may be, has been proved to the satisfaction of the Court or the Registrar, as the case may be.

Appendix D

(5) In any case to which section 10(2) of the Act applies the Court may adjourn the application for registration until such enquiries as it makes or as it causes to be made are completed and may give such direction in relation to any enquiries which it thinks appropriate as appear necessary in the circumstances of the case.

(6) In any case in which a valid notice of objection to the registration has been given or for other sufficient reason the Court may require such party objecting to the registration to file an affidavit or affidavits in support of the grounds of objection and the person concerned shall comply with the directions of the Court in relation to such matters. Notice of objection shall, as far as practicable, be in the Form No. 3 or No. 4 as the case may be.

(7) In any case in which it appears necessary in the interests of justice to the Court to do so, it may direct that an issue or issues arising in relation to an application for registration or an objection thereto be heard on oral evidence and may give such directions concerning the exchange of pleadings, or the making of discovery as appear necessary and proper in the circumstances of the case.

(8) In any case in which an objection to an attorney or to a power is established but an enduring power subsists as respects an attorney who is not affected thereby, the Court shall direct the registration of the enduring power of attorney by qualifying the registration by specifying in its order that the power concerned shall not be exercisable or shall be exercisable subject to conditions or, as the case may be, that the attorney concerned shall not exercise or purport to exercise the power originally intended to be granted and the power of attorney shall thereafter be subject to such qualification as is specified in the order.

Post Registration Applications

4(1) Subsequent to the registration of an instrument an application:

> (a) to disclaim a power pursuant to section 11(1)(b) of the Act, or
>
> (b) for the exercise by the Court of any power conferred by section 12(2) to (6) inclusive of the Act;

shall be made by notice of motion to the Court and shall be lodged in the Office of the Wards of Court. Such motion shall as far as practicable be in the Form No. 2 as set out in the Appendix hereto and shall be grounded upon the affidavit of the moving party which shall fully set forth the facts and circumstances giving rise to the making of the application.

(2) The provisions of sub rules 2 to 9 inclusive of rule 3 shall apply *mutatis mutandis*, where applicable, in relation to any application brought under this rule.

The Registrar

5(1) The Registrar shall keep and maintain a Register in which he shall register all instruments which are entitled to be registered as an enduring power of attorney under the provisions of the Act. Such Register shall record the date of application for registration, the date of registration, any qualification specified by the Court in relation to a registration and any applications with regard to the revocation or cancellation of the registration of an instrument.

(2) The Registrar shall maintain a cause book in which all applications made under the Act in relation to any enduring power of attorney (whether registered or unregistered) and the outcome of same shall be recorded. Such cause book shall only be available for inspection by the applicant, the donor, any person on whom a relevant notice has been served or such other person as the Registrar may, in his discretion, permit.

(3) The Registrar shall keep and retain in the Office of the Wards of Court an attested copy of all enduring powers of attorney lodged with him for the purpose of registration or which are lodged in Court for the purposes of any application under the Act and shall supply attested copies to any person entitled to same pursuant to section 11 of the Act.

(4) The Registrar may, in any case in which it appears appropriate to do so, issue a certificate certifying that an application for registration has been made but not yet determined or that an application has been made which has resulted in the registration of the instrument to which it relates and such certificate may be given in the Form No. 5 in the Appendix hereto as may be appropriate.

Costs

6. The costs of any application to the Court or any objection to any application shall be in the discretion of the Court.

S.I. NO. 66 OF 2000

RULES OF THE SUPERIOR COURTS (NO. 1)

(POWERS OF ATTORNEY ACT 1996) 2000

We, the Superior Courts Rules Committee, constituted pursuant to the provisions of the Courts of Justice Act, 1936, section 67, and reconstituted pursuant to the provisions of the Courts of Justice Act, 1953, section 15, by virtue of the powers conferred upon us by the Courts of Justice Act, 1924, section 36, and the Courts of Justice Act, 1936, section 68 (as applied by the Courts (Supplemental Provisions) Act, 1961, section 48), and the Courts (Supplemental Provisions) Act, 1961, section 14, and of all other powers enabling us in this behalf, do hereby make the annexed Rules of Court.

Dated this 20th day of April, 1999

Liam Hamilton
Frederick Morris
Ronan Keane
Kevin Lynch
Richard Johnson
Harry Hill
Eamon Marray
Edward Comyn
Gordon Holmes

Appendix D

I concur in the making of the annexed Rules of Court

Dated this 8th day of March, 2000

John O'Donoghue

Aire Dli agus Cirt

Comhionannais agus Athchoirithe Dli

INDEX

Accounts
    attorney keeping, 7, 9, 37
Alzheimer's disease
    sufferers from, 3
Attorney
    accounts, keeping, 7, 9, 37
    appointment by donor, 7
    authority,
        conditions or restrictions, 10–12
        scope of, 10–12
    bankruptcy of, 8, 9
    effect of accepting enduring power, information on, 40, 47, 48
    enduring power, as donee of, 5
    gifts of property of donor, making, 10–12
    joint, 34, 35
    joint and several, 20, 21, 35
    mismanagement by, 16
    notices to, 34
    offence against person of donor, conviction of, 8
    personal care decisions by, 8, 11, 12
    qualifications of, 7
    registered power invalid or not in force, protection on, 18–20
    registration, application for, 13, 14
    remuneration, 37
    substitute, power to appoint, 8

Bankruptcy
    attorney, of, 8, 9

Company
    statutory declaration by, 4
Convey
    meaning, 4
Conveyance
    power of attorney, under, 23, 24
        revocation, protection on, 24–27

Donor
    enduring power, of,
        affairs of, meaning, 5
        attorneys, appointment of, 7
        mental capacity,
            opinion of medical practitioner as to, 7, 9
            presumption as to, 5
        mentally incapable, becoming, 2
        notices to, 33, 34, 38, 46
        personal care decision,
            attorney, by, 8, 11, 12
            meaning, 5, 6
            power to make, 5
        personal representative, as, 12
        power of attorney, of, signature, 22, 23

Enduring power of attorney
    application for relief, information in affidavit grounding, 62, 63
    attorney. *See* **Attorney**
    characteristics of, 6–10
    coming into force, 12, 13
    common law jurisdictions, in, 2
    disclaimer, 8
    effect of accepting, information on, 40, 47, 48
    effect of creating, information on, 38, 39, 46, 47
    execution, notice of, 37, 38
    High Court, applications to, 61–63
    instrument creating,
        execution, 23, 37
        form of, 38–45
        personal care decisions, for, 46–52
    introduction in England and Wales, 2
    invalidation, 8, 9, 19
    notice of execution, 9, 37, 38

Index

Enduring power of attorney—*contd.*
  personal care decisions,
    instrument creating power for, 46–52
    regulations, 57–59
  persons executing, 9
  post registration applications for, 68
  pre-registration applications for, 66
  provision for, 2
  registered medical practitioner, statement by, 45, 52
  registered,
    functions of court, 17, 18
    invalidity, protection of attorney and third party, 18–20
    not in force, protection of attorney and third party, 19–20
  registration. *See* **Registration of enduring power**
  regulations, 6, 7, 9
  revocation after registration, 16, 20
  solicitor, statement by, 45, 52
  spouse, in favour of, 8–10
  statements in, 7
  stock exchange transaction, protection of transferee under, 27
  survival of, 12, 13

High Court
  applications to, 61–63
  Central Office, deposit of instrument creating power of attorney in, 29, 30
  jurisdiction, 5, 6
  registered power, functions relating to, 17, 18

Houses of Oireachtas
  orders and regulations laid before, 30

Mental incapacity
  donor of power, of, 2
  existence of, 3
  meaning, 5, 6

Nursing home
  owner,
    attorney, not to be, 7, 8
    meaning, 8

Personal care decisions
  attorney, by, 8, 11, 12
  instrument creating power for, 46–52
  meaning, 5, 6
  power to make, 5
  regulations, 57–59

Personal representative
  donor as, 12

Power of attorney
  creation of,
    formalities for, 22
    statutory provisions, 4
  donee,
    execution of instruments by, 23, 24
    revocation of power, protection on, 23–26
    stock exchange transaction, protection of transferee under, 26, 27
  donor. *See* **Donor**
  general,
    effect of, 22
    form of, 36
  instrument creating,
    Central Office, deposit in, 29, 30
    proof of, 28, 29
    purchaser of estate or interest in land, furnishing to, 30
  meaning, 4
  proof of, 28, 29
  revocation,
    common law, at, 26
    donee, protection of, 24–27
    purchaser, protection of, 24–27
  security, given as, 27, 28

Registration of enduring power
  administrative basis, on, 6
  application for, 13, 14, 66–68
  cancellation by court, 17, 18
  committee appointed under Lunacy Regulation, where, 15, 16

Registration of enduring power—
contd.
effect of, 16
functions of court prior to, 13
functions of court after, 17
Judge of High Court, application
   to, 6
meaning, 5
mistakes made during, 9
notice of intention to apply for,
   54, 55
notices prior to,
   contents of, 33
   donor, to, 31
   form of, 38, 53
   other attorneys, to, 34
   persons to whom given, 31–33
register, 68
registrar, 68, 69
objection to, 14–16

Registration of enduring power—
contd.
procedure, 14–16
proof of, 16
refusal of, 15

Securities
transfer, protection of transferee,
   27

Security
power of attorney as, 27, 28

Spouse
enduring power in favour of,
   8–10

Statutory declaration
company, by, 4
meaning, 4

Wardship
jurisdiction, 3